D0712368

ONE CENTURY LATER

ONE CENTURY LATER

WESTERN CANADIAN RESERVE INDIANS SINCE TREATY 7

Edited by

Ian A. L. Getty and Donald B. Smith

UNIVERSITY OF BRITISH COLUMBIA PRESS

VANCOUVER

ONE CENTURY LATER

WESTERN CANADIAN RESERVE INDIANS SINCE TREATY 7

Publication has been made possible in part by grants from
the University of Calgary Research Policy and Grants Committee
and from the Intellectual Prospecting Fund.

Canadian Cataloguing in Publication Data

Western Canadian Studies Conference, 9th, University of
Calgary, 1977.
    One century later

    Bibliography: p. 188
    ISBN 0-7748-0103-4 bd.
    ISBN 0-7748-0105-4 pa.

    1. Indians of North America—The West, Canadian
—Congresses. 2. Indians of North America—The
West, Canadian—Government relations—Congresses.
I. Getty, Ian A. L., 1947- II. Smith, Donald B., 1946-
III. Title.
E78.C2W48 1977   971.2'004'97   C78-002194-0

International Standard Book Number
(Hard cover edition) 0-7748-0103-4
(Paper cover edition) 0-7748-0105-0

Contents

Illustrations

Photographic Credits

Plate 31 is from the Vancouver City Archives. Plates 32, 33, and 34 appear courtesy of Selwyn Dewdney. All other plates and the cover photograph are from the Glenbow–Alberta Institute.

Preface

While there is today an increasing interest in Canada's native peoples, there is a chronic shortage of scholarly books and articles written about them. The demand, in fact, has become so great that the University of Toronto Press recently reprinted in paperback Diamond Jenness's *Indians of Canada*, which first appeared in 1932. How ironic that this volume should be reissued in a decade when Indians have the highest rate of natural increase in Canada, for Jenness believed, like many of his generation half a century ago, that the Indian was a "vanishing race." "Doubtless all the tribes will disappear. Some will endure only a few years longer, others like the Eskimo, may last several centuries (p. 264)." It is tragic that academics have so neglected the study of Canada's native peoples that we are obliged to depend on such outdated studies.

Recognizing the need for reliable source materials on the Western Canadian Indian, the Department of History of the University of Calgary chose the history of the native peoples as the subject of its 9th Annual Western Canadian Studies Conference in 1977. Since 1977 marked the hundredth anniversary of the signing of Treaty Seven, by which present-day southern Alberta was surrendered to the Crown by the Blackfoot, Blood, Peigan, Sarcee, and Stoney Indians, we decided to entitle the conference "One Century Later: The Native Peoples of Western Canada since the 'Making' of the Treaties," and we asked our participants to treat an aspect of the "reserve period" in their papers.

As several of the opening speakers commented, one of the most important topics to be researched is the history of the implementation of the treaties. There are, for example, few detailed studies on the federal government's Indian policy in the twentieth century. This lack is puzzling, both because there has been enormous documentation produced in this century by the Department of Indian Affairs, which is readily available in the Public Archives of Canada, and because these voluminous records can be supplemented by the oral testimony of hundreds upon hundreds of "experts" on Canada's Indian policy in the early twentieth century—native elders who have lived through it. As Chief John Snow and Dr. Joseph Couture pointed out in their introductory remarks, there is at present an excessive dependence on the written history of the native peoples. Oral tradition is an untapped resource, and, as Dr. Couture added, "as a point of professional integrity, historians must come to grips with the issue of the accuracy of native oral history, in order, as a *sine qua non*, to develop more comprehensive understanding and appreciation of that history."

Within the broad topic of federal Indian policy itself there are numerous topics that cry out for further study, such as the promises that were made to provide adequate educational facilities, the government's obligations concerning the native peoples' health and welfare, and the Crown's administration of Indian lands. Investigations into the Department of Indian Affairs' educational system might help to explain the inability of many native people today to compete and to reside in the non-Indian world around them. A detailed investigation of native health and welfare should also be undertaken. Canada's Indian population might well have been declining in the first years of this century, as Diamond Jenness pointed out, but it should now be determined whether this was a result of the government's neglect of proper health care for its Indian wards. All of these questions arise from the remarks of the lieutenant-governor of Alberta and the leaders of the Treaty Seven tribes.

Lieutenant-Governor Ralph Steinhauer, himself a Treaty Indian, opened the conference. In his address he made the initial suggestion that perhaps the non-native society had failed to live up to the treaty promises of 1877. Looking out over the crowded hall, filled with over five hundred native and non-native students, teachers, and members of the public, he commented:

> One hundred years later at a conference like this, there are no tipis in evidence but look at the building we are in [MacEwan Hall on the University of Calgary campus]. What a change! And such a large gathering of people, and not all Indians. This is an indication to me that something is bothering your conscience a hundred years later and you are here today to see if you can help the native rectify some of the things that might have been mistakes that day or might have been oversights.
>
> Whether they are mistakes or oversights, I hope that this conference will be able to bring together and help the native people perhaps understand you a little better, but more than that, to help you to understand the native people in their own right a little better.

In their words of welcome the Treaty Seven leaders—Councillor Rufus Goodstriker of the Bloods, Chief Bill McLean of the Bearspaw band of the Stoneys, Chief Nelson Small Legs, Senior, of the Peigans, Chief John Snow of the Wesley band of the Stoneys, and Chief Leo Pretty Young Man of the Blackfoot—made it clear that for them the anniversary of the treaty was a commemoration, not a celebration. As Chief Snow stated: "are we ... celebrating the highest unemployment rate in Alberta? Are we also celebrating the lack of housing, the lack of social services, the lack of proper educational facilities, the problems of alcoholism, and the loss of our treaty rights?" The comments of the Treaty Seven leaders provide a forceful reminder of the native peoples' concern about the government's honouring of the terms and the spirit of the treaties.

These proceedings contain the formal texts submitted after the conference. The address by Chief John Snow, "Treaty Number Seven Centennial: Celebration or Commemoration?", opens the volume, and an eloquent statement by Harold Cardinal, then president of the Indian Association of Alberta, "Treaties Six and Seven: The Next Century," concludes the collection. The academic papers delivered at the conference are divided into two sections: the historical and the contemporary. Each section covers a varied range of topics reflective of the diversity of Canada's native peoples, and the papers cover geographically all of the Western provinces. Within each essay are suggestions for many future articles and books on the native peoples in the post-treaty era.

The historical section is opened by Arthur Ray's essay, "Fur Trade History as an Aspect of Native History." In his article Professor Ray provides a general overview of the Western Canadian Indian's involvement in the fur trade before the "making" of the treaties. In contrast to those who argue that the native peoples were "exploited" by the traders, he suggests that they were "astute traders and consumers." His paper goes far towards making the Western Canadian Indian a three-dimensional figure, a man who had his "own clearly defined sets of objectives and conventions for carrying on exchange with the European." The monopolizing position of the Hudson's Bay Company did not result in windfall profits, and the Indian–trader relationship itself was a complex interchange of cultural and economic values.

In the second article, "One Hundred Years of Treaty Seven," Hugh Dempsey reviews the recent history of the native peoples of southern Alberta. Dr. Dempsey takes the story of the five tribes who assembled to sign Treaty Seven at Blackfoot Crossing from the early reserve period to the present day. He demonstrates how the Blackfoot and Blood tribes successfully adjusted to farming, only to be defeated when full-scale mechanization was introduced after the First World War. Lacking the capital to modernize, many Indian cattlemen and farmers fell behind the rest of society in the 1920's and 1930's. Today, as Dr. Dempsey concludes, the Indian people face the new challenge of adjusting to a rapidly expanding, industrialized urban society.

The paper by Professor Stan Cuthand on "The Native Peoples of the Prairie Provinces in the 1920's and 1930's" highlights some of the social, economic, and political developments of the Plains Indian in the interwar decades. His review of conditions on the Western reserves points to the deteriorating position of the native peoples in the early twentieth century. "Conditions on Indian reserves in practically every area—social services, health, education, and living facilities," he writes, "had deteriorated in the years since the signing of the Treaties." But at the same time, the Cree academic adds, there was a ray of hope, for it was also during this time that the modern pan-Indian movement arose in Western Canada under the leadership of the Six Nations (Ontario) war veteran, Lieutenant Frederick O. Loft, who founded the League of Indians of Canada in 1919. Loft's circular letters to tribal leaders across Canada provide an excellent summary of the League's goals. In addition, the minutes of the resolutions passed at League meetings during the 1920's and 1930's provide further insight into the pressing concerns of the Prairie Indians. In the 1940's the Indian Association of Alberta and the Federation of Saskatchewan Indians were formed, to a certain extent on the political foundations laid by the earlier League of Indians of Canada.

E. Palmer Patterson's paper, "Andrew Paull and the Early History of British Columbia Indian Organizations," complements the discussion of the growth of political organizations on the Prairies. Focusing upon the life of Andrew Paull, the Squamish native leader, as the central thread of his narrative, Professor Patterson relates the history of native organizations on the Pacific Coast in the early twentieth century. From his paper it becomes quite evident how much further advanced the Pacific coast tribes were in political organization in the 1920's and 1930's than were those on the Prairies. As Patterson clearly establishes, it was largely thanks to men like Paull, who had a firm grounding in both the Euro–Canadian and the Indian cultures, that such progress was made in establishing Indian organizations in British Columbia.

The final paper in the historical section is a case study of one Indian group in Western Canada: the Sioux or Dakota. It should be noted that the author, G. F. G. Stanley, wrote his first book dealing with Canada's native peoples, *The Birth of Western Canada* (1936), over forty years ago. In his paper, "Displaced Red Men: The Sioux in Canada," Professor Stanley chronicles the history of the refugee Sioux who fled north after the Minnesota uprising of 1862 and the Battle of Little Big Horn in 1876. They received temporary sanctuary in Western Canada, and despite the government's policy of peaceful removal, a small minority never returned to the United States. Their descendants, as Dr. Stanley explains, still live today on reserves granted to them in Saskatchewan and Manitoba. Like many bands across Canada, the various Sioux communities in Saskatchewan and Manitoba are presently researching the history of their people in order to document their rights and privileges under the treaty agreements and the Indian Act. An important problem facing the federal government today is whether these bands, and other native bands in northern Alberta and Saskatchewan who claim to have been overlooked at the signing of the original treaty negotiations, should now sign adhesion to the existing treaties.

The contemporary section of the volume is introduced by an interesting quantitative analysis by Professors Roger Gibbins and Rick Ponting of the University of Calgary. In 1976, Gibbins, a political scientist, and Ponting, a sociologist, completed a survey of Euro–Canadian perceptions of the Western Canadian Indian. They summarize their findings in their paper, "Prairie Canadians' Orientations towards Indians," and, contrary to pre-conceived notions often portrayed by the news media, they discovered that the general population was receptive towards the working out of a new accommodation between the two groups.

If Western Canadian attitudes have really changed, as Gibbins and Ponting state, and the non-Indian populace is ready to respect the Indians' "distinctiveness," one wonders why the federal government continues to work towards what Marie Smallface Marule terms the elimination of "any special status for Indians and Indian lands." In her paper, "The Canadian Government's Termination Policy: From 1969 to the Present Day," she strongly attacks "the paternalistic and colonial nature of the administration of Indian Affairs." As Professor Marule was the executive assistant to the president of the National Indian Brotherhood in the early 1970's, her paper reflects many of the concerns of Canada's native leaders in responding to the "White Paper" of 1969. Her essay is a cogent blend of research with the first-hand account of a direct participant.

Leaving the political sphere, the final two papers are devoted to culture and education. Selwyn Dewdney provides a fascinating glimpse of the world of Western Canadian Indian art today. In his paper, "Birth of a Cree–Ojibway Style of Contemporary Art," he relates how the Ojibway artist, Norval Morrisseau, has inspired an entire generation of native painters since the early 1960's. Dewdney observes that Morrisseau and his contemporaries have provided in their work "evidence of the growing strength of peoples whose deeper identities it has been impossible to suppress." The new Cree and Ojibway artists use their own native styles and have been influenced primarily by their own cultural traditions and legends, not by those of the dominant society.

This same sense of vitality is present in the philosophy and oral tradition of the native elders. Joseph Couture stresses their importance in his essay, "Philosophy and Psychology of Native Education." He notes that the elders have an extraordinary gift to "draw out, to develop human potential." In direct contrast to those who scorn the retention of the old ways, he urges that the wisdom of the elders be incorporated into the formal education process for native students today.

The final address of the conference, "Treaties Six and Seven: The Next Century," was given at the banquet on Saturday evening. The guest speaker, Harold Cardinal, first reviewed the last one hundred years to provide a better understanding of what must be done in the next century. "If there is one mistake that was made in the past," he began, "it was that we trusted too much." It is the duty of each succeeding generation, he concluded, to ensure that the sacred obligations of the treaties are respected. It was on that note of vigilance that the conference, "One Century Later," formally ended.

Our warmest thanks are given to all those individuals and organizations that contributed to the conference's success: to the Stoney Tribal Council, the Stoney Cultural Educational Programme, and to Chief John Snow for kindly inviting all the delegates to the Morley Reserve thirty miles west of Calgary for a pow wow on the Friday evening of the conference; to the University of Calgary Native Students Club, in particular Louise Loyie, the club president, and Josy Pakes, a member of the club's executive, for all their assistance with the general organization of the conference, and for the programme at the Saturday evening banquet at the Calgary Convention Centre; to Lieutenant-Governor Ralph Steinhauer for opening the conference, and to the official representatives from the Treaty Seven tribes for their words of welcome; to Professors Eugene Dais of the University of Calgary, Leslie Green of the University of Alberta, LeRoy Little Bear of the University of Lethbridge, and President Lloyd Barber of the University of Regina, for participating in the panel "Native Peoples and the Law"; to the staffs of the Conference Office, the Department of History, the Faculty of Social Sciences, all of the University of Calgary; to those sending displays: the Public Archives of Canada, the Alberta Provincial Museum, and the various publishers; and to the funding agencies: The Canada Council and the University of Calgary Research Grants Office. It is hoped that these proceedings will, in a permanent way, help to further the exchange and the dialogue which began among the several hundred native and non-native delegates on 18–19 February 1977.

Donald B. Smith
Ian A. L. Getty

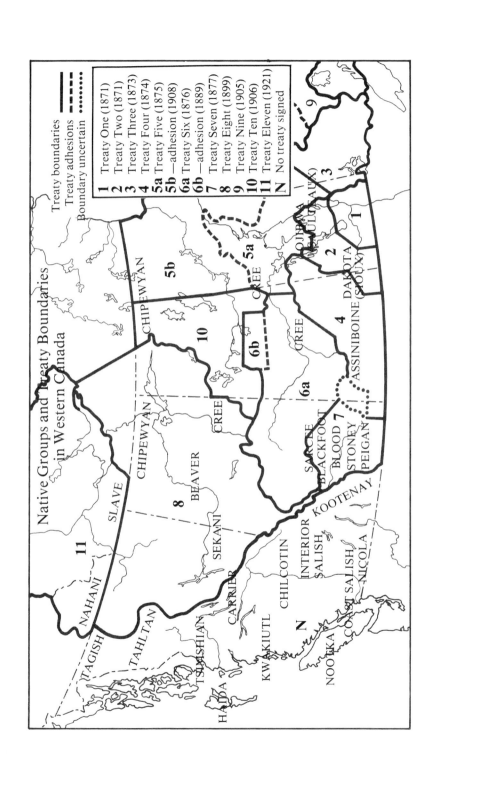

Native Groups and Treaty Boundaries
in Western Canada

Treaty boundaries
Treaty adhesions
Boundary uncertain

1   Treaty One (1871)
2   Treaty Two (1871)
3   Treaty Three (1873)
4   Treaty Four (1874)
5a   Treaty Five (1875)
5b   – adhesion (1908)
6a   Treaty Six (1876)
6b   – adhesion (1889)
7   Treaty Seven (1877)
8   Treaty Eight (1899)
9   Treaty Nine (1905)
10   Treaty Ten (1906)
11   Treaty Eleven (1921)
N   No treaty signed

TAGISH
NAHANI
11
TAHLTAN
SLAVE
CHIPEWYAN
CHIPEWYAN
5b
TSIMSHIAN
HAIDA
SEKANI
8
BEAVER
CHIPEWYAN
10
CREE
CARRIER
CREE
KWAKIUTL
CHILCOTIN
N
INTERIOR
SALISH
6a
KOOTENAY
SARCEE
BLACKFOOT
BLOOD 7
STONEY
PEIGAN
NOOTKA
COAST SALISH
NICOLA
CREE
ASSINIBOINE
4
CREE
5a
6b
CREE
OJIBWA
(SAULTEAUX)
DAKOTA
(SIOUX)
2
1
3
9

1

Treaty Seven Centennial:
Celebration or Commemoration?

CHIEF JOHN SNOW

I stand before you today as one of the descendants and a member of the Stoney Tribe, one of the tribes which signed a peace treaty known as Treaty Seven, concluded one hundred years ago. I am proud as I stand before you one century later, because I represent an honest people. I am proud because I represent the honest party of those who signed Treaty Seven one hundred years ago. But I cannot use the word "honest" for the Queen's representatives, the federal government, and the missionaries who were involved in the treaty negotiations, treaty promises, and treaty agreement. The word honest is not applicable to them. The terms forked tongue, greed, and land thieves would be more appropriate and fitting for them.

I think it is most appropriate to have the theme "One Century Later" during this ninth annual Western Canada history conference which coincides with the centenary of Treaty Seven. There are many things that I would like to discuss at this conference. Within the time allotted to me I will say a few things that I feel are very important to my people.

The story or the history of Canada started with us Indian people of various tribes. The history books may not say this, but the fact is the story of Canada began with us Indians. We have a very colourful history on this North American continent. We as Indian people belong to this country. We belong to this country just like the mountains, the forests, the prairies, the rivers, lakes, and streams. We belong here just like the buffalo, the antelope, and the thunderbird and eagle belong here. We as Indian people are part of this great country and this great country is part of us. We are part of this beautiful land and this beautiful land is part of us.

We speak the language of this beautiful land. Yes, we speak the original language of this land. We sing the songs and music of this land. We drum and chant the music that is in harmony with nature and in tune with this land.

We have a religion that is indigenous to this land. We believe in the Great

Spirit, the Creator who made this beautiful land. We are the Great Spirit's people. We were the keepers of this land.

One century later we are dismayed, frustrated, and hurt. One century later, we have become strangers in our homeland. Most of our land, our resources, and wealth are taken from us in the name of progress and civilization. One century later, we have become a poor people, a forgotten people in a strange and indifferent society. There is no meaningful redress for our land claims. There is no respect from the uncomprehending larger society for our treaty rights, hunting rights, fishing rights, and aboriginal rights. One century later, we as Indian people have almost lost faith in democracy in a land of democracy. We have been supressed by government red tape, bureaucracy, and paternalism. We have experienced despair, loneliness, and hopelessness.

No one seemed to be really interested in the Indian and his problems. They are only interested in Indian land because it contains a wealth of re-sources, natural resources, water resources, mineral resources, gold, ore, gas, and oil, not to mention the renewable resources and the game popula-tion. A U.S. president once described an Indian reservation this way: he said, an Indian reservation is a land set aside for Indian people surrounded by land thieves. We know exactly what the president meant. One century later, many of our beautiful and living forests have been flooded. Huge hydro dams are built. In many cases no compensation was made for flooding our hunting grounds, sacred areas, and traditional areas. The motto seemed to be, if you step on the Indian without compensation, make a hydro dam, build a skyscraper, because this is progress. In the name of progress there is no redress. In the name of progress we are becoming powerless.

When I reflect on the past one hundred years of our history, I begin to think what is it we are supposed to be celebrating? A celebration should be a festive and happy occasion. But I want to challenge the Canadian public —are we native people also "celebrating" the highest unemployment rate in Alberta? Are we also celebrating the lack of housing, the lack of social ser-vices, the lack of proper educational facilities, the problems of alcoholism, and the loss of our treaty rights? Are we as Indian people celebrating the loss of our beautiful forests, prairies, rivers, lakes, and streams?

Long ago we used to go to the mountain hot springs for healing. We used to gather mountain plants and herbs for medicine. We used to go to the mountains to get natural earth-paints for our ceremonial use. We used to gather pipe-stone for ceremonial purposes. These have now become national parks, provincial parks, wilderness areas, natural areas, with strict legislation barring us Indians from following our traditional religious practices. The hot springs areas have become tourist resorts. These sacred areas have become skiing and resort places for capturing the tourist dollar. Our sacred places are gone.

When the first Europeans came over from the old country, we were told that they were fleeing from wicked men and from religious persecution. They were looking for a land of religious freedom. They found such a place here in North America. They found religious freedom here. What did they do? It was a paradox that is hard for us to understand. These very people who were looking for a land of religious freedom, when they found one quickly enslaved the inhabitants of the land of religious freedom. When they came, our religious freedom ended. The minds of these religious European people were closed. They said, "Ours is the only true religion. Anything that is not written down on paper and that has no dates attached to it is false."

It is important that historians recognize another form of history, the oral accounts of historic events and understandings passed down by the elders of our tribes. Many of you automatically reject this type of history, but that is exactly how misunderstanding, prejudice, and fallacy begin. The white man has this unassailable belief that if something is not written down on paper, it does not count as history. What an incredible perversion and distortion of facts in the name of history. If the oral tradition of my people is not' recognized and receives no credence from historians, then I can no longer have any confidence in the social science discipline called "history."

My tribe will be commemorating the hundredth anniversary of Treaty Seven. I looked up the word "commemorate" in the dictionary of the English language, and commemorate means "to honour the memory with a ceremony." We will honour the memories of our forefathers in a religious ceremony, and we will thank the Great Spirit for our survival as a people in the midst of religious persecution, discrimination, and despair. We have survived at great odds. At one time in history we were called 'the vanishing American.' I thank the Great Spirit that we are still here as a people. The Great Spirit has placed us here on this beautiful land for a purpose. We as Indian people are beginning to rediscover our heritage, culture, language, and religion after one hundred years of being called savage, heathen, drunk, and lazy. We were created for a purpose by the Great Spirit. We are now rediscovering that purpose.

What about the next hundred years? What does the future hold for the Indian people? Within the last decade I have seen a few positive signs, but this is not enough to make a substantial difference in our society. It has been very difficult for us Indian people to break into the establishment.

Do we see Indian people from reserves holding ministerial posts in the federal cabinet or in the provincial cabinet and giving leadership in our country? No! Being a minority group and having limited voting power makes it almost impossible for us to achieve this goal.

Do we see Indian people preparing documents to be introduced and to become legislation and law of this country? One of our elders in the Stoney tribe, Mr. Jake Rabbit, made a comment on this matter. He was discussing the many problems in our society. He said, "an irresponsible younger, meaning the white brother, has come and made all kinds of regulations and laws of this land. He did this without consulting his older brother." We, the elder brother, know this country. We have been here for many hundreds of years. We know the weather, we know the seasons, and we know every trail and mountain pass in this area. We are aware of the laws of the Creator. We know the country. This irresponsible younger brother has made many problems for himself in his society and many problems for us too. He should have consulted his older brother before he got into this mess. I hope that the Indian people will be consulted before any more new legislation is passed in our country.

I have mixed feelings as we enter the second century. I am a little optimistic as we enter the hundredth year of Treaty Seven. I see a few positive signs. One positive sign is the revival of Indian religion. There is a re-awakening of Indian religion, philosophy, and traditional thought and way of life. Although we cannot relive the old days, I am sure that we can use the ancient truth and wisdom of the older chiefs and apply them to our times.

During the past several years there has been a real interest in the Indian Ecumenical Conference. Indian religious leaders, medicine men, ceremonial leaders, clergymen, doctors, university students, and Indian people from all over the North American continent have come many times to the gathering of the tribes at Morley for week-long conferences. Most of the people in attendance are Indian young people who come to listen to the lectures and teachings of the elders. The sayings of the elders are simple and direct, and yet they carry profound and deep insight into religious truth, thought, culture, and way of life. Their teaching is about the Great Spirit, the Creator, and how to walk the straight path and live the good life.

The elders are concerned about the larger society. They are concerned about today's trends of technology and development and the possible ecological consequences that may come about because of them. Development and technology should be guided with the Indian philosophy of living in harmony with nature and in accordance with the creation of the Great Spirit. If we destroy the environment we are destroying ourselves. If we pollute the waters we are destroying ourselves. But if we protect and respect the environment we are ultimately protecting ourselves. If we safeguard waters we are protecting ourselves and our children. Future development should be based not only on how much money we make, but also on conservation and environmental concerns. The real estate man is very uneasy when he sees a vacant lot. He sees dollar signs and skyscrapers. The Indian sees land differently. He does not see all the dollar signs. He is not blinded by the money-making process. He sees the beauty of the land and is thankful for life, thankful for the land the Creator has made for his enjoyment.

I want to call upon the chiefs and councils of Treaty Seven to declare the centennial year as the year to begin negotiations. This year we must clarify the misunderstandings between the government and the Indian people concerning the terms of Treaty Seven. I would like to discuss this year not only the precise wording and fine points of the treaty agreement as contained in the parchment, but also the oral accounts of the negotiations as told by Indian people. Our people say the minerals and the vast natural resources were never discussed at Blackfoot Crossing. The treaty was a peace treaty between Indian tribes and white settlers. The agreement was to share the land. Let us sit down with the government of Canada and clearly spell out and document our understanding of the treaty in all areas where we disagree in interpretation. Instead of having some bureaucrats in Ottawa decide for us, we must make it clear that today we are the negotiators, being descendants of the signatories of the treaty.

I am calling on all treaty Indians of our country to unite and challenge the Canadian government to take seriously the treaties that were made. We as Indian people are prepared during this centennial year to look into the treaties to try and solve our differences. I would also like discussion and clarification regarding the Natural Resources Transfer Act of 1930 whereby our vast resources were transferred from the federal government to the province. I would like to see a meeting of the federal and provincial governments and treaty Indians regarding this matter.

We must plan a good future for our children. We, the descendants of those who signed Treaty Seven, now have the opportunity, during this centennial year, not only to reflect back but also to look forward to the next hundred years—to renegotiate, interpret, and clarify the terms of the treaty as understood by our forefathers. We must safeguard and protect our treaty rights, because it was agreed that both parties would honour the treaty as long as the sun shines, grass grows, and the rivers flow.

In closing I would like to say this in Indian traditional style.

O Great Spirit, whose voice I hear in the winds, like the thunderbird of old let me rise above the mountain top. Give me the wings of inspiration and strength to rise again, to rise above my present problems of despair and hopelessness!

O Great Spirit, let me walk in beauty and in dignity on this beautiful land once more. Like the olden times I shall go to the mountain top to pray. Perchance I will see a vision. I shall look for the wisdom of the old chiefs. I shall look for the courage of the brave warriors. I shall look for the pride of my people. I shall look for the religion that once cloaked this vast continent!

When I have rediscovered these things which are essential for a nation to survive and to rise, then out of the depth of despair and hopelessness of the past, out of the ashes of the past, and, like the thunderbird of old, my people shall rise. We shall find the purpose to which we were created. Like the days of old we shall govern and take our place with wisdom, courage, pride, and dignity in the modern society!

Then there will be a great celebration by our people on this land! Even our Mother Earth will rejoice on that day! The prairies, the forest, the mountains, the animals and birds, and all living things on North America shall rejoice!

I look forward with confidence to the next hundred years. I know the Great Spirit is in control! I know he cares for his red children. I know he cares for our Mother Earth.

Like the Hebrew prophet of old, I will repeat, "They who wait upon the Great Spirit shall renew their strength, they shall mount up with wings as eagles, they shall run and not be weary, they shall walk and not faint."

2

Fur Trade History as
an Aspect of Native History*

ARTHUR J. RAY

Howard Adams, among others, has made the point that the dominant white Euro-Canadian culture has projected racist images of the Indians that, "are so distorted that they portray natives as little more than savages without intelligence or beauty."[1] He argued further that the Indians "must endure a history that shames them, destroys their confidence, and causes them to reject their heritage."[2] There is a great deal of truth in Adams's statements, and clearly a considerable amount of historical research needs to be done to correct these distorted images. One important aspect of any new meaningful Indian history necessarily will be concerned with the involvement of the Indian peoples in the fur trade and with the impact of that participation upon their traditional cultures as well as those of the European intruders. Work in this area will be important not only because it holds a potential for giving us new insights into Indian history, but also because it should serve to help establish Indian history in its rightful place in the mainstream of Canadian historiography. As some of Canada's most prominent historians have emphasized, the fur trade was a molding force in the economic, political, and social development of Canada,[3] and the Indian peoples played a central role in this enterprise. For these reasons Indian history should not simply be devoted to recounting the manner in which the aboriginal peoples of Canada were subjugated and exploited, but it must also consider the positive contribution that the Indian peoples made to the fur trade and, hence, to the development of Canada. If this positive contribution is recognized, it should help destroy some of the distorted images that many Canadians have of Indians and their history.

Given that fur trade history and Indian history are inextricably bound together, several questions immediately arise. How much attention have historians devoted to the roles that the Indians played in the fur trade in the

*I would like to thank Charles A. Bishop, SUNY-Oswego; James R. Gibson and Conrad Heidenreich, York University; and Carol Judd, Ottawa, for commenting on earlier drafts of this paper. The author, of course, is responsible for this paper.

considerable body of fur trade literature that already exists? What images of the Indian peoples emerge from this literature? What aspects of Indian involvement have yet to be explored fully?

Until relatively recently the Indian peoples have not figured prominently in works dealing with the fur trade.[4] Rather, they generally appear only as shadowy figures who are always present, but never central characters, in the unfolding events.[5] In part, this neglect appears related to the fact that historians have been primarily concerned with studying the fur trade as an aspect of European imperial history or of Canadian business and economic history.[6] And, reflecting these basic interests, the considerable biographical literature that fur trade research has generated deals almost exclusively with Euro-Canadian personalities.[7] Relatively few Indian leaders have been studied to date.[8]

Although the tendency to consider the fur trade primarily as an aspect of Euro-Canadian history has been partly responsible for the failure of scholars to focus on the Indians' role in the enterprise, other factors have been influential as well. One of the basic problems with most studies of Indian–white relations has been that ethno-historians and historians have taken a retrospective view. They see the subjugation of the Indian peoples and the destruction of their lifestyles as inevitable consequences of the technological gap that existed between European and Indian cultures at the time of contact.[9] From this technological–determinist perspective, the Indian has been rendered as an essentially powerless figure who was swept along by the tide of European expansion without any real hope of channeling its direction or of influencing the character of the contact situation. The dominance of this outlook has meant that in most fur trade studies the Indian has been cast in a reflexive role. Reflecting this perspective, until recently most ethno-historical research has been approached from an acculturation–assimilation point of view. The questions asked are generally concerned with determining how Indian groups incorporated European technology as well as social, political, economic, and religious customs into their traditional cultures.

While also interested in these issues, historians have devoted a considerable amount of attention toward outlining the manner and extent to which Euro-Canadian groups, particularly missionaries and government officials, helped the Indians to adjust to the new socio-economic conditions that resulted from the expansion of Western cultures into the new world.[10] Often historical research has taken a certain moralistic tone, assuming that members of the dominant white society had an obligation to help the Indians adopt agriculture and European socio-economic practices and moral codes, so that the Indian peoples could fit into the newly emerging social order.[11] Thus, historians who undertake these types of studies are frequently seeking to determine whether or not the traders, missionaries, and government officials had fulfilled their obligations to help "civilize" the Indian.

Granting that much good work has been done in the above areas, it is my opinion that many new insights into Indian history can be obtained if we abandon the retrospective, technological-determinist outlook and devote more attention to an examination of Indian involvement in the fur trade in the context of contemporary conditions. Such an approach would necessarily recognize that the nature of the trading partnerships that existed between Indian groups and various European interests changed substantially over time and place, making it difficult, frequently misleading, and certainly premature, given the amount of research that still needs to be done, to make any sweeping statements at this time about the nature of Indian–white relations in the context of the Canadian fur trade.

In order to pursue this work effectively, two courses of action need to be followed—one is not currently popular, and the other is extremely tedious. First, students of Indian history need to abandon the assumption that the Indians were ruthlessly exploited and cheated in all areas and periods by white traders. At present this is a very popular theme for both Indian and liberal white historians. All of us have heard the story many times of how the Indians sold Manhattan Island for a few pounds of beads, and we have been informed of the many instances when Indians parted with valuable furs for trinkets and a drink. But, why are we never informed of what the Indians' perceptions of trade were? It may well be that they too thought they were taking advantage of the Europeans. For example, in 1634, when commenting on Montagnais beaver trapping in eastern Canada, Father Le Jeune wrote:

> The Castor or Beaver is taken in several ways. The Savages say it is the animal well-beloved by the French, English and Basques,—in a word, by the Europeans. I heard my [Indian] host say one day, jokingly, *Missi picoutau amiscou*, "The Beaver does everything perfectly well, it makes kettles, hatchets, swords, knives, bread; and in short, it makes everything." He was making sport of us Europeans, who have such a fondness for the skin of this animal and who fight to see who will get it; they carry this to such an extent that my host said to me one day, showing me a beautiful knife, "The English have no sense; they give us twenty knives like this for one Beaver skin."[12]

While there is no denying that European abuses of Indians were all too common, there are several things wrong with continually stressing this aspect of the fur trade and Indian history. As the previous quote suggests, it gives us only half the story. Of greater importance, by continually focusing only on this dimension of the trade, we run the serious risk of simply perpetuating one of the images in Indian historiography that Adams, among others, most strongly objects to, namely, the view that the Indians were little more than "savages without intelligence." It also glosses over a fundamental point that must be recognized if the Indian is to be cast in an active and creative role. We must not forget that the Indians became involved in the fur trade by their own choice. Bearing that in mind, an objective and thorough examination of the archival records of the leading trading companies, admittedly a wearisome task, gives considerable evidence that the Indians were sophisticated traders, who had their own clearly defined sets of objectives and conventions for carrying on exchange with the Europeans.

This can be demonstrated by following several lines of inquiry. One of these involves attempting to determine the kind of consumers the Indians were at the time of initial contact and how their buying habits changed over time. Probably one of the most striking pictures that emerges from an examination of the early correspondence books of the Hudson's Bay Company is that, contrary to the popular image, the Indians had a sharp eye for quality merchandise and a well-defined shopping list. In short, they were astute consumers and not people who were easily hoodwinked.

If this is doubted, the early letters that the traders on Hudson Bay sent to the governor and committee of the Hudson's Bay Company in London should be read carefully. A substantial portion of almost every letter deals with the subject of the quality of the company's trade goods and with the Indians' reactions to it. Not only do these letters reveal that the Indians could readily recognize superior merchandise, but they also indicate that the Indians knew how to take advantage of the prevailing economic situation to improve the quality of the goods being offered to them. The following quote, typical of those that were written in the period before 1763, demonstrates the point and at the same time indicates one of the problems that is associated with carrying on research of this type. On 8 August 1728, Thomas McCliesh sent a letter from York Factory to the governor and committee in London informing them:

I have sent home two bath rings as samples, for of late most of the rings [which] are sent are too small, having now upon remains 216 that none of the Indians will Trade. I have likewise sent home 59 ivory combs that will not be traded, they having no great teeth, and 3900 large musket flints and small pistol flints, likewise one hatchet, finding at least 150 such in three casks that we opened this summer which causes great grumbling amongst the natives. We have likewise Sent home 18 barrels of powder that came over in 1727, for badness I never saw the like, for it will not kill fowl nor beast at thirty yards distance: and as for kettles in general they are not fit to put into a Indian's hand being all of them thin, and eared with tender old brass that will not bear their weight when full of liquid, and soldered in several places. Never was any man so upbraided with our powder, kettles and hatchets, than we have been this summer by all the natives, especially by those that borders near the French. Our cloth likewise is so stretched with the tenter-hooks, so as the selvedge is almost tore from one end of the pieces to the other. I hope that such care will be taken so as will prevent the like for the future, for the natives are grown so politic in their way of trade, so as they are not to be dealt by as formerly ... and I affirm that man is not fit to be entrusted with the Company's interest here or in any of their factories that does not make more profit to the Company in dealing in a good commodity than in a bad. For now is the time to oblidge [*sic*] the natives before the French draws them to their settlement.[13]

From McCliesh's letter one gets the impression that few of the goods on hand were satisfactory as far as the Indians were concerned. Taken out of context, comments of this type, which are common in the correspondence from the posts, could be construed to indicate that the governor and committee of the Hudson's Bay Company hoped to enhance their profits by dealing in cheap, poor quality merchandise whenever possible. However, such a conclusion would distort the reality of the situation and overlook important developments that were underway in the eighteenth century. If one examines the letters that the governor and committee sent to the Bay during the same period, as well as the minutes of their meetings in London and correspondence with British manufacturers and purchasing agents, other important facts emerge.

These other documents reveal that from the outset the governor and committee were concerned with having an array of the types and quality of goods that would appeal to the Indians. From the minute books of the company we learn that in the earliest years of operations the London directors relied heavily upon the experience and judgment of Pierre-Esprit Radisson to provide them with guidance in developing an inventory of merchandise that would be suitable for their posts in Canada. Radisson helped choose the patterns for knives, hatchets, guns, and so forth that manufacturers were to use, and he was expected to evaluate the quality of items that were produced for the company.[14] The governor and committee also sought the expertise of others in their efforts to maintain some quality control. For instance, in 1674 they attempted to enlist the services of the gunsmith who inspected and approved the trade guns of the East India Company.[15] They wanted him to evaluate the firearms that the Hudson's Bay Company was purchasing.

In their annual letters to the posts on the Bay, the governor and committee generally asked the traders to comment on the goods that they received and to indicate which, if any, manufacturer's merchandise was substandard. When new items were introduced, the directors wanted to know what the Indians' reactions to them were.

The question that no doubt arises is, if the governor and committee were as concerned with the quality of the products they sold, as suggested above, then why was there a steady stream of complaints back to London about their goods? Before a completely satisfactory answer to this question can be given, a great deal more research needs to be done in these records. However, several working hypotheses may be put forth at this time for the sake of discussion and research orientation. In developing its inventory of trade goods, the Hudson's Bay Company, as well as other European groups, had to deal with several problems. One of these was environmental in character. Goods that may have been satisfactory for trade in Europe, Africa, or Asia, often proved to be unsuitable in the harsh, subarctic environment. This was especially true of any items that were manufactured of iron. For example, one of the problems with the early flintlocks was that the locks froze in the winter.[16]

The extremely cold temperatures of the winter also meant that metal became brittle. Hence, if there were any flaws or cracks in the metal used to make mainsprings for guns, gun barrels, knives, hatchets, or kettles, these goods would break during the winter. In this way the severe environment of the subarctic necessitated very rigid standards of quality if the goods that were offered to the Indians were going to be satisfactory. These standards surely tested the skills of the company's suppliers and forced the company to monitor closely how the various manufacturers' goods held up under use.

Besides having to respond to environmental conditions, the traders also had to contend with a group of consumers who were becoming increasingly sophisticated and demanding. As the Indians substituted more and more European manufactures for traditional items, their livelihood and well-being became more dependent upon the quality of the articles that they were acquiring at the trading posts. This growing reliance meant that the Indians could no longer afford to accept goods that experience taught them would fail under the stress of hard usage and the environment, since such failures could threaten their survival. It was partly for these reasons that the Indians developed a critical eye for quality and could readily perceive the most minute defects in trade merchandise.

Indian groups were also quick to take advantage of competitive conditions. They became good comparison shoppers and until 1821 used European trading rivalries to force the improvement of quality and range of goods that were made available to them. For example, during the first century of trade on Hudson Bay, the Indians frequently brought to Hudson's Bay

Company posts French goods that they judged to be superior to those of English manufacture. The Indians then demanded that the Hudson's Bay Company traders match or exceed the quality of these items or risk the loss of their trade to the French. Similar tactics were used by the Indians in later years whenever competition was strong between Euro-Canadian groups. Clearly such actions were not those of "dumb savages," but rather were those of astute traders and consumers, who knew how to respond to changing economic conditions to further their own best interests. The impact that these actions had on the overall profitability of the trade for Euro-Canadian traders has yet to be determined.

The issue of profits raises another whole area of concern that is poorly understood and should be studied in depth. To date we know little about how the economic motivations of the Europeans and the Indians influenced the rates of exchange that were used at the posts. In fact, there is still a great deal of confusion about the complicated system of pricing goods and furs that was used in Canada. We know that the Hudson's Bay Company traders used two sets of standards. There was an official rate of exchange that was set by the governor and committee in London which differed from the actual rate that was used at the posts. Of importance, the traders advanced the prices of their merchandise above the stated tariff by resorting to the use of short measures. Contemporary critics of the Hudson's Bay Company and modern native historians have attacked the company for using such business practices, charging that the Indians were thereby being systematically cheated, or to use the modern expression, "ripped off."[17] But was this the case? Could the company traders have duped the Indians over long periods of time without the latter having caught on? Again, common sense and the record suggests that this was not the case.

The traders have left accounts of what they claimed were typical speeches of Indian trading leaders. One central element of all of these addresses was the request by these leaders that the traders give the Indians "full measure and a little over."[18] Also, the Indians usually asked to see the old measures or standards. Significantly, the Indians do not appear to have ever challenged the official standards, while at the same time they knew that they never received "full measure." What can we conclude from these facts?

In reality, the official standards of trade of the Hudson's Bay Company, and perhaps those of other companies as well, served only as a language of trade, or point of reference, that enabled the Indians and the traders to come to terms relatively quickly. The traders would not sell goods at prices below those set in the official standard. The Indian goal, on the other hand, was to try to obtain terms that approximated the official rate of exchange. An analysis of the Hudson's Bay Company post account books for the period before 1770 reveals that the company traders always managed to advance prices above the standard, but the margin of the advance diminished as the

intensity of French opposition increased.[19] And even under monopoly conditions such as existed in Western Canada before the 1730's, the Hudson's
Bay Company traders were not able to achieve an across-the-board increase
that exceeded 50 per cent for any length of time.[20] This suggests strongly
that the Indians successfully used competitive situations to improve the
terms of trade and that they had their limits. If prices were advanced beyond
a certain level, the Indians must have perceived that their economic reward
was no longer worth the effort expended, and they broke off trade even
if there was no alternative European group to turn to.

These remarks about the *overplus* system apply to the period before 1770.
What we need to know is the extent to which the Indians were able to influence
the rates of exchange during the time of bitter Hudson's Bay Company and
North West Company rivalry. A preliminary sample of data from that period
suggests their impact was much greater and that range of price variation
was much more extreme than in the earlier years. Similarly, it would be
helpful to have some idea what effect the re-establishment of the Hudson's
Bay Company's monopoly after 1821 had on trade good prices and fur values
in Western Canada. Being able to monitor prices under these contrasting
conditions would enable us to obtain some idea of how the Indians were
coping with the changing economic situation and how their responses influenced the material well-being of the different tribal groups.

Although this sample of the early accounting records shows that the
Indians were economic men in the sense that they sought to maximize the
return they obtained for their efforts, the same documents also indicate
that, unlike their European counterparts, the Indians did not trade to accumulate wealth for status purposes. Rather, the Indians seem to have engaged
in trade primarily to satisfy their own immediate requirement for goods.
On a short-term basis their consumer demand was inelastic. In the early
years this type of response was important in two respects. It was discon-
certing to the European traders in that when they were offered better prices
for their furs, the Indians typically responded by offering fewer pelts on a
per capita basis. This type of a supply response was reinforced by gift-giving
practices. Following the Indian custom, prior to trade tribal groups and
the Europeans exchanged gifts. As rivalries for the allegiance of the Indians
intensified, the lavishness of the gifts that the traders offered increased.

The ramifications that Indian supply responses to rising fur prices and
to European gift-giving practices had for the overall conduct of the fur trade
have yet to be fully explored. Clearly the costs that the Europeans would
have had to absorb would have risen substantially during the periods when
competition was strong, but to date no one has attempted to obtain even
a rough idea of the magnitude by which these costs rose during the time
of English–French or Hudson's Bay Company–North West Company rivalry.
Nor has serious consideration been given to the manner in which such eco-

nomic pressures may have favoured the use and abuse of certain trade articles such as alcohol and tobacco.

Concerning the use of alcohol, the excessive consumption of this drug was an inevitable consequence of the manner in which the economies of the Indian and European were linked together in the fur trade and of the contrasting economic motives of the two groups. As rivalries intensified, the European traders sought some means of retaining their contacts with the Indians, while at the same time keeping the per capita supply of furs that were obtained at as high a level as was possible. However, in attempting to accomplish the latter objective, the Europeans faced a number of problems. The mobile life of the Indians meant that their ability to accumulate material wealth was limited, especially in the early years when the trading posts were distant from the Indians' homelands. And, there were social sanctions against the accumulation of wealth by individual Indians.[21] To combat these problems, the traders needed to find commodities that could be transported easily or, even better, consumed at the trading post.

Unfortunately, alcohol was ideal when viewed from this coldly economic perspective. It offered one of the best means of absorbing the excess purchasing power of the Indians during periods of intensive competition. Furthermore, alcohol could be obtained relatively cheaply and diluted with water prior to trade.[22] Hence, it was a high profit trade item, an article that helped the traders hold down their gift-giving expenses, and it could be consumed at the forts. Given these characteristics, the only way that the abusive use of alcohol in trade could have been prevented in the absence of a strong European or native system of government was through monopoly control.

The traditional Indian consumer habits and responses to rising fur prices were important in another way. They were basically conservationist in nature although not intentionally so. By trapping only enough furs to buy the goods they needed in the early years, the pressures that the Indians exerted on the environment by their trapping activities were far less than they would have been had the objective been one of accumulating wealth for status purposes. If the latter had been the primary goal, then the Indians would have been tempted to increase their per capita supply of peltry as fur prices rose, since their purchasing power was greater.

In light of the above, the period between 1763 and 1821 is particularly interesting and warrants close study. During that period Euro-Canadian trading rivalries reached a peak, and one of the consequences of the cutthroat competition that characterized the time was that large territories were over-hunted and trapped by the Indians to the point that the economies of the latter were threatened.[23] The question is, had the basic economic behaviour of the Indians changed to such an extent that it facilitated their over-killing fur and game animals? Or, was the heavy use of addictive consumables such as alcohol and tobacco a major factor in the destruction of the environment?

Yet another aspect of the fur trade that has received too little attention is the connection that existed between the European and eastern North American markets and the Western Canadian operations of the trading companies. It needs to be determined how prices for trade goods and furs in these markets, as well as transportation costs, influenced rates of exchange at the posts. For instance, it has become popular to cite cases where European traders advanced the prices of certain articles by as much as 1,000 per cent over what it cost the companies to buy them in Europe. Similarly, accounts of occasions when the Indians received a mere pittance for valuable furs[24] are common. But, it is rarely reported, and indeed it is generally not known, what percentage of the total gross revenues of a company were made by buying and selling such items. Nor is it known if losses were sustained on the sales of other commodities. Equally important, there is not even a rough idea of what the total overhead costs of the companies were at various times. Hence, their net profit margins remain a mystery, and what was considered to be a reasonable profit margin by European standards in the seventeenth, eighteenth, and early nineteenth centuries is not known. Answers to all of these questions must be found before any conclusions can be reached about whether or not the Indian or the European trader was being "ripped off."

And indeed, the Indian side must be considered when dealing with this question and when attempting to understand how the trading system responded to changing economic conditions. Even though Harold Innis pointed out that Indian trading specialists played a crucial role in the development and expansion of the fur trade, a common view of the Indians in the enterprise is still one that portrays them basically as simple trappers who hunted their own furs and accepted whatever prices for these commodities that the traders were willing to give them. The fact of the matter is that the records show that in the period before 1770, probably 80 per cent of all of the furs the Europeans received in central Canada came from Indian middlemen who acquired their peltry through their own trading networks.

Furthermore, these middlemen charged the Europeans substantially more for these furs than they had paid to obtain them from the trapping bands with whom they dealt. In turn, the middlemen advanced the prices for their trade goods well above the levels they had been charged by the Europeans, sometimes by margins of almost 1,000 per cent.

These practices of the Indian middlemen raise a difficult question. If the Indians were not engaged in the trade to accumulate wealth, as suggested earlier, then why did the middlemen advance their prices to the extent that they did? Did their price levels simply enable them to maintain a material standard that they had become accustomed to? Before this question can be answered, a great deal more needs to be known about the problems that the Indian middlemen had to cope with in their efforts to acquire and transport goods and furs. A clearer understanding of their motives for engaging in the trade is also required. For example, why did some Indian groups quickly assume the middleman role while others were apparently content to continue as trappers? How did middlemen groups fare, economically, in comparison with trapping groups?

The Indians played a variety of other roles in the fur trade. They served as provision suppliers, canoe builders, canoe and boat men, and farm labourers around the posts, to name only a few. The Indians quickly assumed these roles as economic conditions changed, rendering old positions obsolete and opening up new opportunities.

This brings to mind another broad research area that should be explored more fully than it has been to date. It deals with determining how the various Indian groups perceived and responded to changing economic situations. Work in this area would serve to destroy another distorted image that many Euro-Canadians have of Indian societies, namely, the view that these societies are rigid and incapable of responding to change. Historically there is little evidence to support such a notion for the period before 1870. While the fur trade was a going concern and the Indians were not tied to the reserves and shackled with bureaucratic red tape, they made many successful adaptations to new circumstances. More needs to be written about this aspect of Indian history. If this work is done, perhaps a picture will emerge that shows the Indians to be innovative, dynamic, and responsive people, whose creativity and initiative have been thwarted in the post-treaty period.

In conclusion, this paper has focused upon the early phases of the Western Canadian fur trade, and the discussion has been restricted primarily to the economic dimension of trade. However, this restriction is justified because many of the problems of Indian–white relations are rooted in the past. Also, many of the distorted images that Euro-Canadians currently hold regarding Indians, thereby causing problems in the relationships between the two groups, have been generated and perpetuated by the manner in which the fur trade history has been written. Correcting these images requires starting at the beginning, and it is not simply a matter of rewriting what has already been done. New research has to be conducted in the various archival collections across the country and records that have received little attention to date, such as accounting records, need to be exhaustively explored. In conducting this research and presenting our results, the urge to overcompensate for past wrongs and inaccuracies by placing the Indian on a pedestal must be resisted. If the latter course of action is taken, a new mythology that will not stand the test of time will be created. Even more serious, it would probably serve only to perpetuate the warped images that such research set out to destroy, because it would fail to treat the Indians as equals with their own cultures and sets of values. Finally, if one of the objectives of studying the fur trade is to attempt to obtain a better understanding of Indian–white relations, it must be based on solid objective historical research.

Notes

[1]Howard Adams, *Prison of Grass* (Toronto: New Press, 1975), p. 41.
[2]Ibid., p. 43.
[3]The most notable example was probably Harold Innis. See H. A. Innis, *The Fur Trade in Canada* (1930; reprint ed., New Haven: Yale University Press, 1962), pp. 386–92.
[4]See, for example, Innis, *The Fur Trade*; A. S. Morton, *The History of the Canadian West to 1870–71*, 2nd ed. (Toronto: University of Toronto Press, 1973); and E. E. Rich, *The Fur Trade and the Northwest to 1857* (Toronto: McClelland and Stewart, 1967).
[5]C. Jaenen, *Friend and Foe* (Toronto: McClelland and Stewart, 1976), pp. 1–11.
[6]Innis and Rich deal extensively with the fur trade as an aspect of imperial history. See Innis, *The Fur Trade*, p. 383; and Rich, *Fur Trade and Northwest*, pp. xi and 296. Several corporate histories have been written. See as examples, L. R. Masson, *Les Bourgeois de la Compagnie du Nord-Ouest*, 2 vols. (1889–90; reprint ed., New York: Antiquarian Press, 1960); E. E. Rich, *The History of Hudson's Bay Company 1670–1870*, 2 vols. (London: Hudson's Bay Record Society, 1958–59); and W. S. Wallace, *Documents Relating to the North West Company* (Toronto: Champlain Society, 1934).
[7]One of the problems, of course, is that biographical details regarding Indian personalities are few. The historical record often does not provide information regarding births, deaths, and family relationships of Indian leaders.
[8]There are some notable exceptions such as Dempsey's study of Crowfoot and Sluman's of Poundmaker. See H. Dempsey, *Crowfoot: Chief of the Blackfoot* (Edmonton: Hurtig, 1972); and N. Sluman, *Poundmaker* (Toronto: McGraw-Hill Ryerson, 1967).
[9]This point of view was perhaps most strongly expressed by Diamond Jenness. See Diamond Jenness, "The Indian Background of Canadian History," Canada, Department of Mines and Resources, National Museum of Canada Bulletin No. 86 (Ottawa, 1937), pp. 1–2; and Diamond Jenness, *Indians of Canada*, 6th ed. (Ottawa: National Museum of Canada, 1963), p. 249. See also George F. Stanley, "The Indian Background of Canadian History," Canadian Historical Association, *Papers* (1952), p. 14.
[10]A notable example of this interest as it pertains to Western Canada is the early work of Frits Pannekoek. See Frits Pannekoek, "Protestant Agricultural Missions in the Canadian West in 1870" (M.A. thesis, University of Alberta, 1970). More recently, Pannekoek has begun to consider the divisive role these groups played in terms of race relations in Western Canada. See Frits Pannekoek, "The Rev. Griffiths Owen Corbett and the Red River Civil War of 1869–70," *Canadian Historical Review* 57 (1976): 133–49.
[11]A notable exception to this viewpoint is that expressed by Stanley in 1952. He pointed out that programmes oriented towards assimilating the Indians into the dominant white society lead to cultural extinction of the former group. This is offensive to any people having a strong sense of identity. See Stanley, p. 21.
[12]R. G. Thwaites, ed., *The Jesuit Relations and Allied Documents*, vol. 6 (New York: Pagent Book Company, 1959), pp. 297–99.
[13]K. G. Davies, ed., *Letters from Hudson Bay, 1703–40* (London: Hudson's Bay Record Society, 1965), p. 136.
[14]E. E. Rich, ed., *Minutes of the Hudson's Bay Company, 1671–74* (Toronto: Champlain Society, 1942), pp. 26–27, 58–59.

¹⁵Ibid., p. 91.

¹⁶A. J. Ray, *Indians in the Fur Trade* (Toronto: University of Toronto Press, 1974), p. 75.

¹⁷For example, in the eighteenth century Arthur Dobbs charged that the company advanced the prices of its goods above the Standards of Trade to such an extent that it discouraged the Indians from trading. Arthur Dobbs, *An Account of the Countries Adjoining to Hudson's Bay in the Northwest Part of America* (London, 1744), p. 43. More recently the company has been attacked for its pricing policy by Adams, *Prison of Grass*, p. 24.

¹⁸C. E. Heidenreich and A. J. Ray, *The Early Fur Trades: A Study in Cultural Interaction* (Toronto: McClelland and Stewart, 1976), pp. 82–83.

¹⁹A. J. Ray, "The Hudson's Bay Company Account Books As Sources for Comparative Economic Analyses of the Fur Trade: An Examination of Exchange Rate Data," *Western Canadian Journal of Anthropology* 6, no. 1 (1976): 44–50.

²⁰The principal exception was at Eastmain where the prevailing rates exceeded the 50 per cent markup level from the late 1690's until about 1720. However, it should be pointed out that French opposition was relatively weak in this area. See Ray, "Hudson's Bay Company Account Books," pp. 45–50.

²¹For example, one of the virtues of Indian leaders was generosity. And, generalized reciprocity or sharing was practised amongst band members. These values and practices served to discourage any individual, regardless of his position, from accumulating wealth in excess of that of his kinsmen.

²²Generally, alcohol was diluted with water by a ratio of one-quarter to one-third at the Hudson's Bay Company posts in the eighteenth century. See Davies, *Letters from Hudson Bay*, p. 268.

²³Ray, *Indians in the Fur Trade*, pp. 117–24.

²⁴Adams, *Prison of Grass*, p. 51; and Susan Hurlich, "Up Against the Bay: Resource Imperialism and Native Resistance," *This Magazine* 9, no. 4 (1975): 4.

3

One Hundred Years of Treaty Seven

HUGH A. DEMPSEY

In 1877, the last of the great Prairie treaties was signed when the warlike tribes of the Blackfoot confederacy and their age-old enemies, the Stoneys, came together to negotiate Treaty Seven with representatives of the Canadian government. In the cool autumn days of late September, they gathered within the protected valley of the Bow River, at Blackfoot Crossing, for the historic occasion. More than ten thousand horses grazed on the hillsides while on treaty flats, hundreds of tipis of the Blackfoot, Blood, Peigan, and Sarcee tribes blanketed the ancient campsite of the Prairie warriors. Across the river, the more docile Stoneys were camped with their Methodist missionary, the Reverend John McDougall and with Hudson's Bay Company traders from Edmonton.

It was a picturesque scene, as revealed through the paintings of Mounted Police surgeon Richard B. Nevitt and through the word pictures of men like Cecil Denny[1] and Richard Hardisty.[2] Yet it was more than just a colourful event, for behind the façade of scarlet tunics, feathered headdresses, and eloquent speeches was the tragedy of a dying nomadic culture. There was also misplaced faith, suspicion, and misunderstanding.

When the government of Canada acquired possession of the territory of Rupert's Land in 1870, it moved quickly to extinguish the claims of its native inhabitants. Following the pattern of earlier agreements in Ontario, the authorities negotiated Treaties One and Two in the Red River area in 1871 and then followed with a series of treaties which by 1876 had reached six in number, and included the vast prairies and woodlands of central Alberta and Saskatchewan.

The reasons for the treaties were simple and straightforward. On one hand, the government wanted to settle with all Indians and métis so that surveyors, railroad companies, and—most important—the settlers, could enter undisturbed. The government had already experienced one problem in being prevented from building a telegraph line west of Battleford before negotiating Treaty Six.[3]

At the same time, many officials subscribed to the idealistic view of

"British justice," and while they may have been willing to circumvent it at times for administrative or pecuniary advantage, it was a very real element in Victorian life. The Canadian government was still morally bound to adhere to the principles set down in the Royal Proclamation of 1763 which required that "the several Nations or Tribes of Indians with whom We are connected, and who live under our Protection, should not be molested or disturbed in the Possession of such parts of our Dominions and Territories as, not having been ceded to or purchased by Us, are reserved to them... as their Hunting Grounds."[4]

In a practical sense, Canada wanted to conclude treaties throughout the fertile regions of the Prairies as soon as possible. It had made a commitment to British Columbia to build a transcontinental railway, and inherent in that pact was the need to provide huge land grants to railway companies and to offer some assurance that Prairie colonization would. be a viable consequence of the project.

By the end of 1876, the only area in the fertile belt not included in a treaty was the vast fifty thousand square mile region of what is now southern Alberta. Bounded roughly by the Red Deer River in the north, the Cypress Hills in the east, the International Boundary to the south, and the Rocky Mountains on the west, it was the traditional hunting grounds of some ten thousand Blackfoot, Blood, Peigan, Sarcee, and Stoney Indians. To deal with these tribes, the government appointed two commissioners, the Honourable David Laird and Colonel James F. Macleod. Laird, who was lieutenant-governor of the North-West Territories, was clearly the political spokesman of the two, while Macleod, the commissioner of the North West Mounted Police, was there because of the tremendous respect which he commanded from the Indians.

The treaty itself was a relatively straightforward document. In exchange for giving up their hunting grounds and promising to live in peace, the Indians were offered reserves on the basis of five persons per square mile; annual treaty money; the right to hunt on crown land subject to later regulations; annual ammunition money; a chief's uniform every three years; a medal, flag, and rifle for the chiefs; cattle, on the basis of two cows per family of five, plus a bull to the chief; tools and a few other sundry items; and a promise to send teachers among them. After a number of delays and discussions, the treaty was finally signed on 22 September.

In retrospect, there can be little doubt that the Indians and the commissioners went to the negotiations with different ideas as to why the meeting had been called. While the government was interested only in negotiating a land treaty, the Indians believed the session was being held to answer their complaints about the métis and Cree hunting buffalo on Blackfoot lands and to deal with the problems of traders and settlers using land and firewood without paying compensation.

In fact, many of the Indians considered the treaty to have been similar to the type they had been making for generations with fur traders and other tribes. Bad Head, who kept the winter count for the Blood tribe and who signed the treaty, thought so little of it that he did not even record it as the main event of the year. Rather, he listed 1877 as *Itsiparkap-otomiop*, or the year "when we had a bad spring."[5]

Any thought that a treaty could be made whereby they could give up the land would have been inconceivable. The Blackfoot, like many other tribes, had no concept of land ownership in the legal sense. To them, one could no more give away the land than the clouds, the wind, or the mountains. It was all part of nature and part of themselves. Rather, they went to the negotiations to seek a solution to their short range problems of hunting rights and the incursion of local traders. Their feelings were best expressed two years later by Father Constantine Scollen, who was present at the signing of the treaty:

> Did these Indians, or do they now, understand the real nature of the treaty made between the Government and themselves in 1877? My answer to this question is unhesitatingly negative, and I stand prepared to substantiate this proposition.
>
> It may be asked: If the Indians did not understand what the treaty meant, why did they sign it? Because previous to the treaty they had always been kindly dealt with by the Authorities, and did not wish to offend them; and although they had many doubts in their mind as to the meaning of the treaty, yet with this precedent before them, they hoped that it simply meant to furnish them with plenty of food and clothing... every time they stood in need of them; and besides this, many outside influences were brought to bear upon them; but I repeat, they were not actuated by any intuitive comprehension of what they were called upon to do.[6]

Nevertheless, Treaty Seven was signed, largely because of the presence of Colonel Macleod as one of the commissioners. As Red Crow, head chief of the Bloods, stated, "Three years ago, when the Police first came to the country, I met and shook hands with Stamixotokon [Colonel Macleod] at Belly River. Since that time he made me many promises. He kept them all—not one of them was ever broken. Everything that the police have done has been good. I entirely trust Stamixotokon, and will leave everything to him. I will sign with Crowfoot."[7]

But almost as soon as the ink was dry on the document, bad luck began to befall the Blackfoot. That autumn, because of the warm dry weather, prairie fires ripped across the open ranges, driving the buffalo south. Before spring, many Indians were feeling the pangs of hunger. To add to their uneasiness, three of the chiefs who signed the treaty were dead within a year. These were Rainy Chief, a head chief of the Bloods, Weasel Bull, and Heavily Whipped. To the Blackfoot, this was a sign that they were being punished. As Father Scollen expressed it:

> Being very superstitious, they often attribute to the white-man any misfortune that may befall them shortly after they have had any dealing with him; and so the death of three of their Chiefs during the first year, alarmed them considerably, and was looked upon as a very bad omen for the future. . . . Since the conclusion of the treaty the decrease of the buffalo has been more apparent than ever before, and during the winter just past, the sufferings of the Indians from hunger have been something unparalleled heretofore in this section of the country. This of course to the Indian mind, is the terrible consequence of the treaty.[8]

Then, as though to confirm the Indians' worst fears, the situation rapidly deteriorated. The buffalo, which Commissioner Laird predicted would last another ten years, were virtually gone from Canada by 1879, and the Blackfoot were obliged either to follow the remaining herds into Montana or to accept the inadequate rations from the unprepared government. By the spring of 1881, even the Montana herds were gone and the Blackfoot had no recourse but to go to the reserves they had chosen and to place their future existence in the hands of the Queen.

As long as there had been buffalo, the Blackfoot were a people to be feared and respected. It gave them an economic base which, coupled with their reputation as warriors, permitted them to display an air of arrogance and independence which did not go unnoticed by the bureaucrats. But by 1881, the rapid changes had drastically affected the position of the tribes of Treaty Seven. Not only were the buffalo gone, thus placing the Blackfoot in the position of having to accept rations, but also their whole nomadic culture had been destroyed. The buffalo had not only supplied food, but also provided leather for clothing and lodges, bones for tools, and a basis for their religion.

In addition, Colonel Macleod had retired as commissioner of the North West Mounted Police, leaving the Indians to discover that this man of honour was not necessarily representative of all policemen or all civil servants. And, with their administration transferred from the Mounted Police to the Department of Indian Affairs, the Blackfoot soon found themselves dominated either by politically appointed Easterners who had little knowledge of the Indians or by local men of questionable character who were willing to work for salaries which were far below the average being paid on the frontier.

Thus the tribes of Treaty Seven entered the decade of the 1880's as indigent mendicants whose very lives depended upon the munificence of the Canadian government. They were difficult years, marked by a sedentary life in tiny cottonwood cabins, the ignominy of accepting weekly rations of beef and flour, unsuccessful attempts to introduce gardening and farming, and a high mortality rate through tuberculosis, measles, scrofula, and venereal disease. As noted by missionary John Maclean,

> The new mode of life on a reserve, dwelling in filthy houses, badly ventilated, has induced disease; the idle manner of living, being fed by the Government, and having little to do; the poor clothing worn in the winter; badly cooked food; [gives] the consciousness that as a race they were fading away.[9]

Of the five tribes, the Stoneys appeared to be faring relatively better than the others. Their economy had been based only partially upon the buffalo, with moose, elk, and deer forming a significant portion of their diet. With the disappearance of the buffalo, the Stoneys became accustomed to using their reserve as a base, but they continued to wander through the foothills from Crowsnest Past to Kootenay Plains. Their ability to support themselves was duly recorded, and during an economy drive in 1884, the Stoneys were cut off from government aid. As the Indian Agent reported,

> I explained to them that the Government considered that they were able to support themselves by hunting and by their increase of cattle, and their land not being suitable for farming the rations were cut off from all, with the exception of the widows, and infirm.[10]

Yet the self-sufficiency of the Stoneys was more illusionary than real. Many families with sick or elderly members remained on the reserve while others worked for nearby ranchers. And even those who did hunt often faced a shortage of food, particularly when the construction of the Canadian Pacific Railway drove much of the game farther afield. Before the end of the decade, the government had been forced to relax its regulations and to issue rations to any Stoneys who applied.

The dream of the government in the 1880's was to make the Indians self-sufficient as quickly as possible. Farming was believed to be the easiest and best way to achieve this goal, regardless of soil conditions or the proclivity of the Indians towards agriculture. At first, many young men and some of the chiefs willingly co-operated in the venture, but the short-sighted pro-grammes usually lacked both planning and understanding.

On the Peigan Reserve, for example, the Indians harvested 2,900 bushels of potatoes in 1882, keeping only enough for their own needs and selling the remainder at two and a half cents a pound. Heartened by this success, the government urged the Peigans to plant more and more until in 1885 they harvested 6,700 bushels only to find they were a glut on the market. By the end of this year their potatoes were selling for less than a half cent a pound and the Indians were discouraged and disillusioned.

Similarly, the Peigan agent learned in the early 1880's that the reserve was unsuited for grain farming because of early frosts, but in spite of one crop failure after another, the Indians were encouraged to keep farming in order to keep them occupied. The agent noted that "the preparation of the ground was a wholesome—though discouraging—occupation for the Indians; the seed grain was literally thrown away."[11]

Many officials honestly felt that the Indians could never survive the transition from their nomadic life and that as tribes they would literally disappear from the face of the earth. The objective, then, was to make them as comfortable as possible during their last days. The old traditional Indians who could not adapt would die; those who became self-sufficient would eventually cease to be Indians and would be absorbed into the larger community. Such an attitude, of course, placed no emphasis upon long range planning.

By the 1890's, the philosophy of self-sufficiency was still alive, but it was apparent to even the most hide-bound bureaucrat that farming was not the only answer. A few Indians were successfully raising small crops of wheat, barley, turnips and, potatoes, but many had neither the desire nor the inclination to work with the soil.

Accordingly, a major programme was introduced in the early 1890's to encourage individual cattle ranching. Prior to that time, band herds had been a source of beef for rations, but ranching was not an individual enter-prise.

On the Blood Reserve, the government offered to trade horses for cattle in 1894. Although horses were still a symbol of wealth, four of the leaders agreed to the exchange. Red Crow and Crop Eared Wolf each took fifteen head, while Blackfoot Old Woman and Sleeps on Top took ten head each. This became the nucleus of the Blood cattle industry which, by the end of the decade, totalled some fifteen hundred head.

Cattle raising was much more acceptable to many Indians than was farm-ing. There were a number of parallels between ranching and their old life, including the fact that the four-footed creatures were bovine relatives of the buffalo, and the Indian rancher could spend many hours in the saddle looking after his herd.

The 1890's also marked the emergence of individual enterprise on some of the reserves. Among the Bloods, a man named Chief Moon took a hay contract in 1891, borrowing equipment from the agent. Within two years, he owned his own equipment and was competing with white ranchers for contracts from the Mounted Police and the Indian Department. Similarly, Heavy Gun started a coal mine on the Blood Reserve in 1892, hiring his own native teamsters and miners, while on the Peigan Reserve, Big Swan opened a stopping house on the stage coach route between Fort Macleod and Pincher Creek.

Each such case was held up as evidence that the Indians could indeed become self-supporting. No mention was made of the scores of others who had become dispirited, dejected, and demoralized by life on the reserve. They had learned to survive on the meagre rations but saw no future ahead for themselves or their children. In fact, with the rise of Indian residential schools, their children were taken away for the greater part of their youthful lives.

In addition, the churches worked actively to replace native practices with Christianity, often without realizing that religious beliefs were inextricably bound with many aspects of their everyday lives. The Reverend John Maclean was aware of this relationship and in 1892 he offered his fellow missionaries a cold and calculated solution:

Missionaries toiling for the welfare of the Indian race are confronted with customs different from their own, and these must be studied, so that wise measures may be adopted for the silent overthrow of all those that are injurious to the advancement of the red man. The sudden change that comes over the mind and heart of the Indians by submission to the Divine, compels a rejection of many customs that are detrimental to their ultimate civilization. Still, there are some that remain that must be gradually undermined by the introduction of influences and counter-customs, before the end is reached which we desire.[12]

As if the internal pressures from the missionaries to convert them and the Indian agents to "civilize" them was not enough, the Indians faced an added problem at the turn of the century when their vacant lands were eyed covetously by incoming settlers. Yielding to political pressures, the government revised the Indian Act in 1907, making it simpler for bands to surrender their reserves. As the deputy superintendent-general stated:

So long as no particular harm nor inconvenience accrued from the Indians holding vacant lands out of proportion to their requirements . . . the department firmly opposed any attempt to induce them to divest themselves of any part of their reserves. Conditions, however, have changed and it is now recognized that where Indians are holding tracts of farming or timber lands beyond their possible requirements and by so doing seriously impeding the growth of settlement ... it is in the best interest of all concerned to encourage such sales.[13]

The Indians of Treaty Seven, occupying some of the largest reserves in Canada, were soon subjected to pressures to surrender parts of their lands. In 1909, the government forced a vote on the Peigan Reserve and in spite of claims of fraud, 28,496 acres of the reserve were sold by the end of the year. Similarly, the Blackfoot succumbed to government pressures, selling 60,771 acres in 1912 and another 55,327 acres in 1918. The Sarcees surrendered only a few acres for a military camp, while the Bloods refused to give up an acre.[14] The land-poor Stoneys, on the other hand, were in a situation where they required more reservation land, rather than giving up what they had.

It is true that the huge land sales added materially to the Indian band funds, the Blackfoot realizing more than $2 million for about half their reserve. Although some of the money was used to build homes and provide other amenities, much of it went to pay for costs normally incurred by the government, such as issuing rations and constructing agency buildings. In the end, those reserves which surrendered lands showed no noticeable advancement or long-term benefits over those which did not.

Yet the situation during this period was not entirely negative. Many students, particularly the sons of chiefs or leading farmers, profited by their years in residential or industrial schools, returning to their reserves to engage in farming on a level comparable to neighbouring white farmers. Others found employment with the Indian agency or on nearby farms, and lived in large, well-furnished homes.

Yet many Indian Department employees considered the task of making their wards self-sufficient to be an impossible one. As an Indian agent stated in 1915:

They are intensely superstitious, and hard to wean away from their pagan beliefs and practices. The great problem to solve for the present generation is to teach them to work. Manual labour will do more than any other single agency to civilize them, and obliterate their nomadic and pleasure-loving habits.[15]

By that time, the Indians of Treaty Seven had experienced almost forty years of paternalism under which the Indian agent had dominated their lives.

Rations, which should have been used as an inducement to work, had just the opposite effect. The use of firearms was restricted. Travel was limited, and anyone leaving his reserve required a pass. The marketing of grain and hay was strictly regulated, and everywhere an Indian turned, he was greeted by limitations and restrictions to his freedom. In the end, it was easier for many to continue the welfare pattern established during the early starvation years than it was to break out of the mòld to make a viable living on the reserve.

It has been said that civilization went into the First World War in wagons and came out in tanks. The whole period from 1914 to 1918 saw a massive shift towards mechanization, and in the years following the war, this change was reflected in many aspects of Canadian society. Soon, the horse-and-plough style of farming was replaced with tractors, threshers, and combines, the farmer becoming a mechanic, businessman, pharmacist, and agrologist.

As long as farming had remained relatively simple, the Indians were able to compete with non-Indian farmers. But when the conversion was made to larger acreages, with mechanized equipment, bank loans, and a knowledge of modern business techniques, the average Indian had neither the education nor the type of cultural heritage to compete. And as he slipped farther and farther behind his white neighbours, his life took on an almost timeless quality. For the next two decades, the Indians of Treaty Seven neither progressed nor regressed. Their population, which reached a low point of less than three thousand after the 1918–19 flu epidemics, rose slightly over the years, but they lived almost as though the world had passed them by. Farming and ranching activities plodded along; children entered and were discharged from residential schools; Christianity seemed to be making headway, but the Sun Dance continued unabated each summer; and the Indian agent ruled supreme, with the chiefs and councils often being little more than figureheads in the decision-making processes.

When the Great Depression struck in 1929, many Indians were barely aware of it. Their lives already were so marginal that the economic stagnation suffered by the rest of Canada was merely a continuation of what the Indians had been experiencing for several decades.

The major change in this pattern occurred immediately following the Second World War. In 1944, just before the end of the conflict, Indian Association of Alberta organizer, Malcolm T. Norris, wrote to his president, John Callihoo:

The time has come in my opinion where the Indians of Alberta may reasonably expect a far better hearing than they have in the past. Everybody realizes today that we will all have to change our social structure for something better than what existed in the past. Any movement for social reform in Canada would be a farce if it did not include Indians since they comprise the great element needing reform.[16]

True to his predictions, the changes came. The first was the opening of the Charles Camsell Indian Hospital in Edmonton in 1945 to combat the deadly killer, tuberculosis. Soon scores of Indians from Treaty Seven were being treated in the capital city. Shortly after, the government changed its policy of discouraging education beyond the age of sixteen years and gradually phased out the church-operated residential schools.

At the same time, the newly formed Indian Association of Alberta became a political force, and although hostilities existed between the Cree locals in the north and the Blackfoot ones in the south, the Treaty Seven tribes took a strong leadership role in the organization. Partly through their efforts, such services as old age pensions and family allowances were extended to treaty Indians.

By the early 1970's, many direct results of the political and educational changes were evident. More and more young college-trained Indians became involved in band administration, and councils assumed greater responsibility for their own affairs. Indian Department administrators discreetly retreated from the reserves to the nearby cities of Calgary and Lethbridge, and the Indian agent became an anachronistic memento of the past. Such industries as a garment factory, prefabricated home factory, commercial wilderness park, golf course, summer resort, and moccasin factory became established on Treaty Seven reserves, and a trend developed towards the retention and preservation of native cultural heritage.

In 1977, an Indian looking back over the past century saw a seemingly endless stream of short-sighted policies, callousness, and neglect. At the same time, he might also have seen many well-meaning people—missionaries, Indian department employees, nurses—who were dedicated to the belief that the only way the Indian could survive in Canadian society was to cast aside all things "Indian" and adopt the practices of the larger society. As one Indian agent stated, it was much easier to have hindsight than foresight.

On the hundredth anniversary of Treaty Seven, the Indians are still burdened with massive problems of unemployment, alcoholism, social breakdown, and a realization that much of their culture has been lost. New problems such as overcrowding, loss of identity, and the rise of urban Indian ghettos are an indication that as old problems are solved, they are soon replaced with new ones. The last hundred years have been difficult, but during the next century, the Indians of Treaty Seven should have a greater role in dealing with their own destiny. That, at least, should count for something.

Notes

[1]Cecil Denny, *The Riders of the Plains* (Calgary: The Herald, 1905), pp. 97–102.

[2]Richard Hardisty, "The Blackfoot Treaty," in *Alberta Historical Review* 5, no. 3 (1957): 20–22.

[3]See Allen Ronaghan, "Three Scouts and the Cart Train," in *Alberta History* 25, no. 1 (1977): 12–14.

[4]Cited in James J. Talman, *Basic Documents in Canadian History* (Toronto: Van Nostrand, 1959), p. 35.

[5]Hugh A. Dempsey, *Blackfoot Winter Count* (Calgary: Glenbow–Alberta Institute, 1965), p. 16.

[6]C. Scollen to A. G. Irvine, 13 April 1879, Indian Affairs Branch file 14924, Ottawa.

[7]*The Globe*, 30 October 1877.

[8]Scollen to Irvine.

[9]John Maclean, *Canadian Savage Folk* (Toronto: William Briggs, 1896), p. 302.

[10]Magnus Begg to Indian Commissioner, 19 May 1884, Indian Affairs Branch file 12349, Ottawa.

[11]Report of R. N. Wilson, Peigan Agency, 22 September 1898, in *Annual Report of the Department of Indian Affairs for 1898*, p. 160.

[12]John Maclean, *The Indians of Canada, Their Manners and Customs* (London: Charles H. Kelly, 1892), p. 272.

[13]Cited in the submission of the Indian Association of Alberta to the *Joint Commission of the Senate and the House of Commons on Indian Affairs, Minutes of Proceedings & Evidence*, no. 3, Ottawa, 11–13 May 1960, p. 128.

[14]R. N. Wilson, "Our Betrayed Wards," *The Western Canadian Journal of Anthropology* 4, no. 1 (1974): 21–31.

[15]Report of W. J. Dilworth, Blood Agency, in *Annual Report of the Department of Indian Affairs for 1915*, p. 78.

[16]Malcolm F. Norris to John Callihoo, 10 February 1944. In author's possession.

4

The Native Peoples of the Prairie Provinces in the 1920's and 1930's

STAN CUTHAND

Following the First World War, new social and political trends began to appear in Canadian society. The Indian people of Western Canada shared in the new political protest movements of the 1920's. The Indians' insight into what was happening and the leaders of their movement for self-determination came from native volunteers who had been in the armed forces. They came home to reactivate Pan-Indianism and to bring about a united effort for better education, ownership of property and land, and improvement in health programmes. The movement towards an organized Pan-Indian movement quickly developed a broader base in Western Canada as other aims concerning treaty and hunting rights, the Indian Act, and economic development became major concerns of all the various bands and tribes.

The first national Indian leader was Lieutenant F. O. Loft,[1] a Mohawk Indian chief from Toronto, who went to London, England, to ask the British Privy Council for a hearing on behalf of the Indians. He was told to organize the Indians before becoming a representative. Working out of his home in Toronto, Loft became president and secretary-treasurer of the League of Indians of Canada which held its first congress at Sault Ste. Marie from 2–4 September 1919.

After the conference Loft drafted a letter to tribal leaders in Quebec, Ontario, and the Prairie provinces, calling for unity to form a body that would be a "power to be heard and their demands recognized by governments." The circular proclaimed:

In politics, in the past they [Canada's Indians] have been in the background....

As peaceable and law-abiding citizens in the past, and even in the late war, we have performed dutiful service to our King, Country and Empire, and we have the right to claim and demand more justice and fair play as a recompense, for we, too, have fought for the sacred rights of justice, freedom and liberty so dear to mankind, no matter what their colour or creed.

The first aim of the League then is to claim and protect the rights of all Indians in Canada by legitimate and just means; second, absolute control in retaining possession or disposition of our lands; that all questions and matters relative to individual and national wellbeing of Indians shall rest with the people and their dealing with the Government shall be by and through their respective band Councils. . . .[2]

One of his first attacks against the Indian Affairs Branch concerned its intention to enfranchise returned soldiers. Loft led a public campaign to have the proposed amendments to the Indian Act dropped because they would result in the "disintegration" of Indian bands.[3]

Although the first organizational meetings were held in Ontario, Chief Loft corresponded from the beginning with leaders in the Prairie reservations. Very few written replies were received and Chief Loft was forced to write to local Indian agents for names of leaders with the ability to read and write English.[4] The first meeting in Western Canada was held at Elphinstone, Manitoba in June 1920. Another meeting was held the following year at Thunderchild Reserve in Saskatchewan. The purpose of these meetings was to seek strength by a united effort to change the suppressive policies of the Indian Affairs Branch and to promote religious freedom and the right to travel without passes.[5]

On 29 June 1922 a conference of Canadian Indians met at the Samson Reserve at Hobbema, Alberta. Over 1,500 Blackfoot, Stoney, Cree, and Assiniboine delegates attended, chiefly from Western Canada. Lieutenant Loft, as president, was known as *Natowew–Kimaw*, "One who speaks for others." The vice-president was Reverend S. A. Bingham from the Walpole Islands, Ontario; the provincial president of Saskatchewan was Reverend Edward Ahenakew; and provincial treasurer was James Wuttunee from Red Pheasant Reserve, Saskatchewan.[7] One of the influential leaders from Alberta was another veteran, Chief Mike Mountain House of the Blood tribe.

Thereafter, the League of Indians met annually in Saskatchewan under the leadership of Edward Ahenakew,[8] the Treaty Six area having the most active membership. Reverend Ahenakew was ideally suited to his position. He had graduated in 1912 from Emmanuel College, the Church of England theological college in Saskatoon, and he had served on numerous Saskatchewan Indian reserves. Sickness forced him to give up his dream of studying medicine at the university in Edmonton, but while he was recuperating from his illness he spent long evenings listening to the Cree elders gathered at Chief Thunderchild's home. Here he learned the old Cree traditions, the stories of Treaty Six and of the 1885 Rebellion, and the difficulties of learning to accept the white man's ways. In *Voices of the Plains Cree* Edward Ahenakew states:

> The principal aim of the League, I would say, is equality for the Indian as citizen—equality, that is, in the two-fold meaning of privileges and responsibility; and to achieve this objective, our first emphasis must be upon improved educational and health programs.... More particularly, the Indians of Canada should have a voice in the character of legislation that is passed in Parliament when it concerns ourselves, for that is the privilege of all under our flag—personal freedom.[9]

Edward Ahenakew worked hard with the League of Indians, in which he served as president for Western Canada. He was also active in the synods of the Anglican Church. Not aggressive in his approach to rectify the wrongs of his people, he was caught between two worlds, and was often more loyal to the Church.

The Indian people liked what Chief Loft had to offer and the movement towards unity was revitalized in 1929 by Chief Joe Taylor at Green Lake, Saskatchewan, when the League of Indians in Western Canada was officially formed. The Saddle Lake Reserve near St. Paul, Alberta, sponsored later conferences in 1931 and 1932. Resolutions were passed in 1931 that on-reserve schools be established to augment industrial and boarding schools, that the old people receive extra rations, that no further land surrenders be made, that Indian hunting, trapping, and fishing rights be preserved, and that a variety of economic assistance programmes be provided by the department to individuals and to bands. There were 1,344 delegates in attendance at the first Saddle Lake convention, including twenty-four chiefs and councillors from thirty Alberta reserves, and twenty-two chiefs and councillors from thirteen Saskatchewan reserves.[10] Augustine Steinhauer was elected president of the Alberta branch of the League of Indians of Canada, and it was his responsibility to help organize the yearly convention and maintain communications with the chiefs and councillors.

The resolutions passed at the 1932 convention at Saddle Lake contained more specific demands. The only one of these to which the Department acceded was a request that only fully qualified teachers be employed in residential and boarding schools. To a resolution that all farm instructors and interpreters be removed from the Alberta and Saskatchewan reserves and that the money saved as a result be used to pay an old age pension to those aged seventy years and older, the Department replied, "It is not likely the Department will assent to getting rid of Farming Instructors.... Increasing relief issues to aged Indians should depend on local conditions." A demand that section 45 of the Indian Act concerning permits be abolished was rejected with the comment that it was "A move for greater freedom of action. The time has not yet come." A general request that the government "abolish the amendments of the Indian Act and . . . follow closely the treaties of 1876 as made by Her Majesty Queen Victoria" received the ill-tempered reply: "Too vague. What amendments are to be abolished? They have all been carefully thought out." Further resolutions concerning individual bands, most of which dealt with land issues and requests for economic assistance, were also ignored.[11]

In 1933 various bands met at Poundmaker's Reserve, Saskatchewan, from 10 to 12 July, and a further meeting was held at Paul's Band near Duffield, Alberta, on 18 and 19 October with Chief Joe Samson from Hobbema elected president of the Alberta League and David Peter from Duffield secretary treasurer.

Many of the issues discussed were carried forward from previous years but often with slightly different point or arguments to make. The 1934 convention was held at Enoch Reserve near Edmonton, and the 1935 convention moved back to Duffield. Some of the more unusual resolutions put forth in these years were:

> That those children who are most advanced in their studies should be sent to a school home where they can mix with the white children. . . .
>
> Resolved that as Canada has freedom of religious worship we Indians would earnestly petition you to grant our request to worship in our own way and according to our past customs the Most High God that created the world and all the beasts thereof and everything that pertaineth thereof, especially as we do not see anything according to our past customs, and especially that we should not be prohibited from holding our ancient Sun Dance, which should be called the Thirsty Dance and the Hungry Dance; a religious ceremony which has been dear to us for centuries and is still dear to us.[12]
>
> That when it is necessary to retain the services of a Doctor other than the doctor retained by the Indian Department, the expense of same shall be met by the Department and not from the Band funds. (This is in accordance with our Treaty). . . .
>
> That where the Reservation boundary linefence extends through or into a lake we shall be given water rights within our line. . . .
>
> That the Department grant a Reservation on Kootenay Plain to the Nordegg Treaty people of Morley Agency.[13]
>
> That as it is now impossible to make a living from hunting and trapping and that we have a large number of Indians on our Reservations who are without the means to farm, we do hereby petition the

Dominion Government through the Department of Indian Affairs, to assist us by providing us with horses, machinery and seed grain. . . .
    That we be given the privilege of choosing our own horses when the Department is purchasing horses for us. . . .
    That as we think it would be in the interest of the Indians to have a committee of their Chiefs and Headmen seated in the House of Parliament during the discussion of Indian matters, we humbly petition you to grant that privilege.[14]
    That the Dept. give us the privilege to rent out new lands to break and cultivate to any white man for five years. The only expense for [the] Indian [is] to furnish posts and get one-third of crop clear annually.[15]

These resolutions are one indication of the problems and difficulties facing Canada's treaty Indians in gaining basic educational and economic assistance and in merely running their day-to-day affairs.
    During the 1930's the League was chiefly concerned with the retention of Indian reserve lands and with the question of ownership of personal property, particularly cattle. They resented the double standard—one for treaty Indians and another for non-Indians—which prevented Indians from selling their cattle. The permit system which restricted travel off one's home reserve still was being enforced by the Department of Indian Affairs. There were only minimal improvements in housing, health services, economic progress and education. The fiftieth anniversary of the signing of Treaty Six passed during the 1920's with little real improvement for Indian people, but now, with the formation of the League, native leaders from across Canada had a national organization to lobby for changes to the Indian Act.

EDUCATION

The educational policy in the 1920's was generally directed towards improving educational facilities, but leaving curriculum content alone. Indian education was administered under the auspices of the Roman Catholic Church and the three Protestant denominations—Presbyterian, Anglican, and Methodist. All the various types of schools were subject to the supervision of the Department of Indian Affairs, because the government provided financial subsidies based on attendance records. The League of Indians was concerned and wanted some improvements because many of the Indian agents were politically appointed, poorly educated white soldiers recently returned from overseas service.
    In 1923 government funding was increased to include all the capital

expenses at Indian residential schools, releasing the finances of the missionary societies and religious orders for better instruction, food, and clothing. Grants were offered to graduates of Indian schools showing academic promise who wished to attend high schools, universities, business colleges, and trade schools. The eligibility requirement stipulated that a student must have passed grade eight by the age of fourteen; but, in fact, many Indian children did not attend school until the age of eight or ten and some started at the age of twelve. Inevitably the programme failed to place many graduates in institutions past the level of grade eight.

During the 1930's increasing emphasis was placed on manual training and vocational instruction in all types of Indian schools. Most of the Indian residential schools included self-sufficient farms of two hundred acres or more with cattle and horses. The school on the Long Plain Reserve near Portage La Prairie had large stables and well-bred stock and sold tons of potatoes every year. It had the first potato planter in the district and had drills for corn, turnips, and grain. In addition, students milked cows and made their own butter. One of the more unusual projects was a mink farm started in 1938 at the Morley Residential School in Alberta. One ill-conceived government plan involved moving the residential schools on the Blood Reserve closer to the town of Cardston, in preparation for having the north part of the reserve surrendered and sold. The Bloods refused to sell, and the controversy created a lot of suspicion among the band members.

There were two schools of thought among white administrators in connection with the education of Indians: boarding the children and teaching them away from their parents; or teaching them on the reserve in day schools in order to influence the reserve by working with the parents. Or to put it another way, some missionary societies said to "Christianize" the Indian first and then "civilize" them; other missionary societies said to "civilize" the Indian first before converting them. There was a rumour among the Indian parents that the only reason the government wanted to teach their children to read and write was to make it easier to train them as soldiers if there was another war. All these attitudes were detrimental to the educational system.

The major problem with day schools was the attendance. From 1909 to 1920, for example, Little Pine Day School near Battleford, Saskatchewan, lists seventeen children, but the attendance ranged anywhere all the way down to zero. The reason for the erratic attendance was the traditional Indian culture. In the fall and spring, families moved to the bush to trap for furs, and during the winter and summer they would move back to the reserve or work on a nearby farm clearing brush. Nevertheless, the residential and day schools contributed greatly to the economy of the reserves by hiring Indians as domestic workers and by purchasing cordwood from local Indian cutters. Attendance was compulsory under the Indian Act, but enforcement varied with each reserve. Some parents wanted their children to attend school in order to understand the white man's ways, but most parents were not willing to force their children to attend school in such an alien environment. Many parents who had been at school felt short-changed by the residential schools under Church control. Those who supported the churches reacted negatively to such a thought. It was a period of division and confusion on many Indian reserves. All the great Indian leaders, like Ahenakew and Steinhauer, were classically educated men, and had read the government documents. At a conference held at North Battleford around 1935 they petitioned the government for improvements in education, health and economic development.

The federal government expenditure for Indian education in 1921 was $1,112,409; but rose to $2,156,882 in 1945; $6,221,792 in 1950; and $31,291,822 in 1964. The cost of Indian education in 1921 was relatively low, because many Indian pupils were enrolled in church-operated schools and less than half of the children of school age were enrolled in any school.

During the years preceding the Second World War, a Special Joint Committee of the Senate and House of Commons made an extensive study of opinion on Indian education. Their report recommended integrated schools wherever possible, with accommodation provided for all Indian children, and decreased enrolment in residential schools. Also, to provide opportunities for vocational and university education, Indian people should assume more responsibility for the education of their own children and become actively involved in school committees.

Progress in Indian education since the 1920's and 1930's has followed many of the proposals put forth during those two decades. In September 1963 R. F. Davey, chief superintendent of Indian education, presented a statement on behalf of the Indian Affairs Branch to the Standing Committee of the Ministers of Education at the Canadian Education Association Convention. His personal observations were that eventually:

1. Indian education should be brought under the jurisdiction of the provinces.
2. Legislation to permit the organization of school units or districts on Indian reserves under provincial authority is required to extend the responsibility of the Indian in the operation of the local school.
3. Legislation [is required] to provide for Indian representation on school boards operating joint schools.
4. Increased provincial control over the integration programme is essential to simplify administration. Federal financial support to the provinces should replace tuition fees payable to local school authorities by the federal government.

5. The Indians must be recognized by the provinces as residents with equal rights and privileges with respect to Indian education.[16]

Edward Ahenakew had made many of the same points as early as 1923.[17] Many of the proposed innovations in Indian education during the 1970's closely resemble these prophetic predictions.

ECONOMIC DEVELOPMENT

Most reserve Indians had horses to sell to the new settlers coming into their area. Many sold dry wood to the farmers and town folk in the winter and hay in the summer. They cut brush most of the summers and were busy with harvesting in the fall. They trapped in the late fall and early spring for muskrats, and during the winter months some trapped weasels, fox, coyotes, and rabbits. Several families gained reputations as good farmers and ranchers.

There were a lot of old-timers past middle age who had never been to school a day of their lives, but who remembered the buffalo hunts way back in 1860, the inter-tribal wars, the warriors' societies, the songs and rituals. Some of them were medicine men. They witnessed the signing of Treaties Four, Six, and Seven and the rebellion of 1885. They passed on their stories and legends at wakes and meetings, and they spoke at dances. They maintained stability in the community. They were proud and independent, preferring to reject or adapt the ideas of the Indian agents and missionaries. These men knew who they were; they reaffirmed their beliefs at sun dances, round dances, horse dances, chicken dances, hand games, the big smoke, and the singing practices. They relived the past in the sacred lodge of the Horn Society. They learned the songs and renewed their bundles.

The old people received their monthly rations from the Indian Affairs —one scoop or two pounds of tea, four pounds of rolled oats, four pounds of salt, one bar of soap, four pounds of rice, one slab of bacon or meat, four pounds of beans, two boxes of matches, twenty pounds of flour, one can of baking powder, and two pounds of lard or tallow. This diet was supplemented by rabbits, ducks, and prairie chickens. They were not too badly off, although at times the old people ran out of tobacco. Under the Veteran's Land Act an amount of up to $2,320 could be granted to an Indian veteran who settled on Indian reserve lands, and the money could be used for specific purposes such as the purchase of livestock, machinery, and building materials.

In the 1930's the older generations came into conflict with the new generation who had been to school. Family-arranged marriages were opposed by the youths, and they often ran away to be married elsewhere. The younger generation refused to accept the traditional role of submitting to the wishes of their fathers and tended to question such traditional customs as giving away horses to visitors. The more educated Indians scoffed at Indian rituals and refused to participate. They danced square dances and quadrilles. They would speak English rather than their native tongue. The more traditional families ignored this and continued to show their Indianness. No matter how far removed they may have been from their hunting, fishing, and food-gathering ancestors, and in spite of opposition from the Indian Affairs policies, the elders continued to renew themselves at the sweat lodges and feasts. They restored relationships and kinship ties at sun dances. When sun dances were completely suppressed by the government, Indians met at exhibitions and fairs to meet each other and renew friendships and strengthen kinship. Kinship was strong amongst the Blackfoot and Crees. Their philosophy was, "Know your relatives and you will know who you are."

HEALTH SERVICES

Working with farm instructors and school teachers were the travelling nurses. Their job was to inspect schools and to go among the homes on the reserves giving assistance and advice. Their efforts met with some resistance. The medicine men and midwives were against the intrusion of white nurses. Often the nurses were driven away from homes. They were often suspected of causing sickness in order to further depopulate the reserves.

Government officials showed a similar misunderstanding of Indian practices. A circular written on 15 December 1921 by Duncan Campbell Scott, deputy superintendent-general of Indian Affairs, gave these instructions to the Indian agents:

It is observed with alarm that the holding of dances by the Indians on their reserves is on the increase, and that these practices tend to disorganize the efforts which the Department is putting forth to make them self-supporting.

I have, therefore, to direct you to use your utmost endeavours to dissuade the Indians from excessive indulgence in the practice of dancing. You should suppress any dances which cause waste of time, interfere with the occupations of the Indians, unsettle them for serious work, injure their health, or encourage them in sloth and idleness. You should also dissuade, and, if possible, prevent them from leaving their reserves for the purposes of attending fairs, exhibitions, etc., when their absence would result in their own farming and other interests being neglected. It is realized that reasonable amusements and recreation should be enjoyed by Indians, but they should not be allowed to dissipate their energies and abandon themselves to demoralizing amusements. By the use of tact and firmness you can obtain control and keep it, and this obstacle to continued progress will then disappear.

The rooms, halls, or other places in which Indians congregate should be under constant inspection. They should be scrubbed, fumigated, cleansed or disinfected to prevent the dissemination of disease. The Indians should be instructed in regard to the matter of proper ventilation and the avoidance of over-crowding rooms where public assemblies are being held, and proper arrangement should be made for the shelter of their horses and ponies. The Agent will avail himself of the services of the medical attendant of his agency in this connection.

The Blood Indians of southern Alberta had a circular log building with no floor at the old Agency, the northern part of the reserve, where they held their dances. They took horses right into the building to give away at honour dances. This building was condemned by the travelling nurses and demolished. On the Little Pine Reserve there was also a circular dance hall where every week during the winter months the people danced. This also was condemned by a travelling nurse, who threatened to set it on fire. The men tore it down. For some years after this the Little Pine Band had no place to dance until Poundmaker's Reserve built their hall. The hall was across the creek and out of sight of government health officials. Periodically, big feasts and dances were held there by the community.

Despite living in what government officials considered to be unhealthy conditions, the overall health of Canadian Indians improved throughout this period. The Canadian native population in 1922 was 100,000—the lowest in history—but in 1923 the superintendent-general, Charles Stewart, reported good progress in matters of health supervision through improved sanitation, and that notwithstanding the ravages of the "flu," the Indian population had been increased to 105,000 for the whole Dominion.

CONCLUSION

The decades between the wars were a period of growth in awareness for native people. In the 1920's the post-treaty generations transferred their identity from that of horsemen of buffalo days to that of cowboys. They wore big hats and neckerchiefs. The ambition of every father was to see his son ride a prancing horse at the sun dance, to ride at horse races, and to ride at a rodeo, like the renowned world rodeo champion Tom Three Persons from the Blood Reserve.

Joe Samson from Hobbema writing in Cree syllabics during the late 1930's speaks of that period, lamenting the fact that the terms of the treaties signed with the Queen's representatives were not kept. The only visible evidence was the school buildings and the farmer instructors' residences. "As far as farming is concerned, I see no sign of real help coming from the Indian Affairs," he wrote. He also lamented that the birds and animals found on the Prairies were becoming less in numbers; some were extinct.

Conditions on Indian reserves in practically every area—social services, health, education, and living facilities—had deteriorated in the years since the signing of the treaties. There was a feeling of frustration, soon to be replaced by hopelessness and despair. But contact with other societies around the world brought a new insight and renewed hope to veterans returning from Europe. The various prairie tribes formed the League of Indians of Canada under the inspiration of Chief Loft, during these two crucial decades. It laid the foundations for the creation of the Indian Association of Alberta in 1939 and of the Federation of Saskatchewan Indians in 1944. As such, it was the first expression of political unity by the Indian people of Western Canada, who began the fight for better services and for a better future.

Notes

[1]Frederick O. Loft was a lieutenant in the Canadian Militia and served overseas from June 1917 to February 1918. He was born at Grand River (Six Nations), Ontario, on 3 February 1872 and was trained as an accountant. He had two brothers, William and Harry. A major source of information on the activities of Chief Loft is found in the Public Archives of Canada, Record Group 10 (Red Series), Volume 3211, file 527787, vol. 1, "Congress of Indians of Canada. General Correspondence, 1919–1935." Also on microfilm C–11, 340.
[2]Circular letter by Chief F. O. Loft, president and secretary-treasurer, League of Indians of Canada, Toronto, 26 November 1919, P.A.C., R.G. 10.
[3]The Toronto *Sunday World*, 6 June 1920; clipping enclosed in P.A.C., R.G. 10. The adverse publicity raised by Loft's activities prompted the deputy superintendent-general of Indian Affairs, Duncan Campbell Scott, to comment: "He has organized a society called 'The League of Indians of Canada,' and he is attempting, I am credibly informed, to work against the administration of the Department, even going so far as to state that he has the ear of the Government and can supersede and circumvent the Department. He is a man of good personal appearance but has no weight, and is endeavouring to work up a reputation for himself. I am particularly anxious that he should not, in any way, be encouraged by the Minister or the Government. At the same time, if he makes any suggestions worthy of consideration, I do not propose to turn them down on account of their source." Memorandum to Mr. Featherston, 28 March 1922; P.A.C., R.G. 10.
[4]Letter addressed to "Dear Brother," dated 25 November 1919; P.A.C., R.G. 10. Some of the correspondents included Teddy Yellow Fly, Blackfoot Reserve; Joe Mountain Horse, Blood Reserve; Dan Wildman, Morley Reserve; and John Barwick, Saddle Lake Reserve.
[5]Ibid.

⁶*Regina Leader* [June/July] 1922; clipping enclosed in P.A.C., R.G. 10. The R.C.M.P. were asked by the Indian Affairs Branch to monitor the proceedings, as well as to prevent any bootlegging of liquor and killing of cattle for meat. The Mounties counted 121 tipis and reported no difficulties during the entire three-day conference. R.C.M.P. "Report Re—Indian League of Nations. Convention at Hobbema. July 3, 1922"; P.A.C., R.G. 10.

⁷The Reverend Canon Edward Ahenakew (1885–1961) was born at Sandy Lake, Saskatchewan, in June 1885. He compiled a series of stories from Chief Thunderchild and recorded some of his own experiences through "Old Keyam." These were edited by Ruth M. Buck in *Voices of the Plains Cree* (Toronto: McClelland and Stewart Limited, 1973). I worked with the editor in providing the Cree translations.

⁸Ibid., p. 186.

⁹Ibid., p. 123–24.

¹⁰"Memorandum of Resolutions passed by the Chiefs, Councillors and Voters of the various Bands of Indians assembled in council at the Convention of the League of Indians of Canada, held at the Saddle Lake Indian Reserve, Alberta, on the 15th, 16th and 17th days of July 1931"; P.A.C., R.G. 10. There are forty-two bands in Alberta and thirty-seven bands in Saskatchewan. Source: *Linguistics and Cultural Affiliations of Canadian Indian Bands* (Ottawa: Department of Indian Affairs and Northern Development, Indian Affairs Branch, 1970).

¹¹"Record and minutes of convention of League of Indians of Canada, Western Branch, held at Saddle Lake Indian Reserve, Alberta, November 3rd and 5th, 1932"; and "Notes on Resolutions of Alberta Branch, League of Indians" [no date, initialled "SC"]; both in P.A.C., R.G. 10.

¹²"*MEMORANDUM* of Resolution passed by the Chiefs, Councillors and members of the various Bands of Indians assembled in council at our convention of the League of Indians of Canada, held at Poundmaker's Reserve in the Province of Saskatchewan near Cut Knife, on July 10th, 11th and 12th, in the year 1933"; P.A.C., R.G. 10.

¹³For an in-depth study of the importance of this resolution, see the book by the Chief of this Stoney Band, John Snow, *These Mountains Are Our Sacred Places* (Toronto: Samuel Stevens, 1977).

¹⁴"Record and Minutes of Convention of the League of Indians of Canada, Western Branch, held at Enoch Reserve July 2nd, 3rd, and 4th, 1934"; P.A.C., R.G. 10.

¹⁵"Records and Minutes of Convention of the League of Indians of Canada, Western Branch, held at Duffield, Alberta Indian Reserve, July 26th and 27th, 1935"; P.A.C., R.G. 10.

¹⁶Ahenakew, *Voices of the Plains Cree*, pp. 186–87.

¹⁷Ibid., pp. 128–29.

5

Andrew Paull and the Early History of British Columbia Indian Organizations

E. PALMER PATTERSON II

The Indian movement in British Columbia emerged out of late nineteenth-century protest concerning Indian land claims. The evolution of the movement into an organized form is associated with several prominent leaders, one of whom is Andrew Paull. In many ways he is the most important figure to study in order to gain an understanding of Indian concerns both in his own day and at present. His life spanned the first half of the twentieth century, he was involved with Indians in a variety of ways—personal and public, local, provincial, and national—and his imagination and vision were the most far-reaching among Indian figures of his time.

In order to understand both Paull and British Columbia Indian affairs, it is necessary to outline briefly these two narratives and to try to link them together. A four-period division of the history of the British Columbia Indian organizations has been proposed by Elizabeth Van Dyke and Douglas Sanders.[1] During the first phase, from the 1880's to 1915, separate Indian communities saw white newcomers arriving in growing numbers. As the settlers came to British Columbia they importuned the government for land. Local Indian groups responded by presenting petitions and sending delegations to Victoria, Ottawa, and London. The main theme of their protest was the European encroachment on the land.

The second period, from 1915 to 1930, saw Indian efforts to organize on a province-wide basis. The Allied Tribes of British Columbia, formed in 1915, sought a settlement of the land claims. This was the first intertribal organization at the provincial level, although not all the tribes were included. It became a training ground for certain individuals who were to continue to play roles in the movement, particularly the Reverend Peter Kelly, a Haida from Skidegate and a Methodist clergyman, and Andrew Paull, a Squamish from North Vancouver. Both were officers on the executive committee. The methods of protest continued to be petitions, memorials, and interviews with provincial and federal officials. White supporters, such as the Friends of the Indians, were consulted and played a contributory role. The Allied Tribes broke up after the Special Joint Committee of the Senate and House of Commons rejected their land claims in 1927.

The third period, from 1930 to 1945, was the era of the birth of the Native Brotherhood of British Columbia. Formed in the Depression when social and economic concerns were uppermost, it turned its attention first to these areas. Individuals, especially Kelly, Paull, and Ambrose Reid, who had been active in the previous decades, reappeared in leadership roles. Other figures whose names are linked to British Columbia Indian history emerged: Alfred Adams, Clifton Heber, Guy Williams, William Scow, William Assu, Dan Assu, and Frank Calder. Primarily an organization of coastal Indians, the Native Brotherhood chiefly emphasized fishing and equal rights issues.

The fourth period, since 1945, saw the birth of the North American Indian Brotherhood, founded and led by Andrew Paull. The Brotherhood, or Paull, argued for special rights for Indians, anticipating the concept of "citizens plus."[2] The organization pressed government for reforms in Indian administration.

Andrew Paull's career illustrates the movement from protest through smaller units to protest through larger units. He embodies the continuity of leadership from the first through the fourth stages of the Van Dyke–Saunders scheme. Indeed, he seemed to anticipate succeeding stages and to provide the additional dimension of proposing an international focus.

Paull's career in Indian public affairs emerged from the context of Oblate missionary activities among the Squamish. Both Catholic and Protestant missionaries had long championed Indian land rights. Early correspondence between Indians and the government of colonial British Columbia reveals the threat to Indian land from incoming whites, who were cutting timber and settling on land reserved for the Indians. Oblate priests, evangelists, and pastors wrote protests on the Indians' behalf.

Intergovernmental rivalry had hindered the progress of Indian land claims. After British Columbia joined Confederation, federal Indian administration was introduced in 1872 in the person of I. W. Powell. He entered into the correspondence over reserve boundary disputes, conflicts with white settlers, and management of funds from reserve lands. Complaints about land, formerly directed to the chief commissioner of lands and works, were now forwarded to the new commissioner for Indian Affairs in British Columbia. Tension between Indian Affairs and the British Columbia government, which was reluctant to cede land for Indian reserves, quickly emerged.

The accuracy of Indian Affairs records about reserves was questioned by the province. Reserves were being expropriated or reduced in size in accordance with the policy established by Joseph Trutch, chief commissioner of lands and works from 1864 to 1871, which allotted a maximum of ten acres to each Indian family.[3] Through the 1860's and 1870's, priests protested and called attention to the potential for violent conflict should grievances over this policy continue. Later, protests from Anglican and Methodist clergy were added to those of the Roman Catholics. Land had become the central issue and the active role of Christian clergy in the controversy had been clearly established. In March 1874, David Laird, minister of the interior (the portfolio for Indian Affairs until 1880), wrote of the dissatisfaction then existing among the Indians of British Columbia due to "the present state of Reserves." He asked for the prompt removal of the source of dissatisfaction, specifically calling for the allotment of eighty acres of land per family.[4]

Although the missionaries supported the Indian cause, their influence produced divisions between Indians based on denominational affiliation. The three main denominations working among British Columbia Indians were the Anglican, Methodist, and Roman Catholic. Historic differences, derived from ancient and modern controversies in Europe, were transported to the mission field. In the case of the Anglicans, the nineteenth-century liturgical reform movement contributed to a further divisiveness, as illustrated by the conflict between William Duncan and Bishops George Hills and William Ridley.

In the interior of British Columbia the Indians were predominantly Roman Catholic, as a result of the work of the Oblates of Mary Immaculate. The southern coastal Indians were also Roman Catholic. The northern coastal people, the Tsimshian, Haida, and Kwakiutl, were Anglican or Methodist. The two Protestant groups gave some lip-service to non-interference and non-competition in the 1870's and 1880's, but they were engaged in a very clear rivalry.

The divisive influence of the missionary is implicit in the view held by some government officials that Methodists were fostering hostility toward the government, while the Anglicans were creating a more friendly atmosphere. The tendency to assign blame to missionaries for the existence of Indian dissatisfaction over the land situation became a regular feature in the years prior to and during the earliest development of Indian organizations. It is itself another example of continuity in the early history of Indian organizations. Reverends Alfred E. Green, Thomas Crosby, William Duncan, Robert Tomlinson, and later Arthur E. O'Meara, whose careers among the Nishga and the Tsimshian cover the period from the 1870's to the 1920's, were all, at one time or another, cited as provokers of discontent.

One example of division along denominational lines can be found in the controversy of claims and counter-claims regarding lands and rights of land usage between the Nishga people of the Methodist mission at Lakkalsap and those at the neighbouring Anglican mission at Kincolith in the 1880's. The Lakkalsap people regarded themselves as having some prior claims because they had lived in the immediate vicinity before the missionaries established Kincolith, a village which drew its inhabitants from a number of other villages. The emergence of the Lakkalsap protest was associated with the Methodist mission led by the Reverend Alfred E. Green. On the other side, the Reverend William Henry Collison, Anglican missionary at Kincolith, was regarded as co-operative and congenial to Indian administration. The differences between Methodist and Anglican Nishga may have existed more in the minds of missionaries and Indian agents than among the Nishga themselves, although the Methodist Indians claimed that the Anglican Indians at Kincolith were as eager as themselves to protest the land claims. George Shankel concludes on the basis of interviews, especially one with the son of reserve commissioner Peter O'Reilly, that in regard to missionary contribution to the protests, the Methodists had only a slight edge over the Anglicans. Several of the figures whose names were associated with protest were from Lakkalsáp, including Chief David Mountain, Arthur Calder, Job Calder, and Charles Russ.

Another dispute, perhaps based on an older and even more traditional rivalry, was that between coastal Tsimshian and Nishga, particularly over certain fishing rights and fishing stations which were located near the mouth of the Nass. It is difficult to speak about this subject with certainty, but it seems that older rivalries and competitions may have been incorporated into new categories introduced by denominational differences.

The debate over two acres of land allotted to the Anglican Church Missionary Society at Metlakatla helped to develop a greater awareness of and sensitivity to the larger threat to Indian land in the province. Here, as on the Nass, the missionaries were in the centre of the controversy. William Duncan, who had been regarded at one time as a genius in bringing Indians to Christianity and Western civilization, was by the mid-1880's regarded as a troublemaker and disturber of the peace. Disenchanted Tsimshians claimed right to the land on which mission buildings stood. The dispute continued until the departure of Duncan and the remaining faithful Tsimshians in 1887 to establish a new community on Annette Island in Alaska.[5]

The protest at Metlakatla inspired other northern claims. Chief Herbert Wallace, a Methodist Tsimshian of Port Simpson, wrote in January 1889, "We want the whole of the Tsimpshean peninsula. We were heathen people once; then we did not know anything about our land, but now we are being civilized, we know this to be our land from our knowledge of God."[6] His remarks seem to substantiate the suspicion that the growing land protest among the Tsimshian was inspired by the missionaries, in this case presumably the Methodist missionary at Port Simpson, the Reverend Thomas Crosby. Crosby and, earlier, his predecessor, the Reverend Alfred E. Green, denied the charge. Green submitted a statement on 17 November 1888, in

Plate 1. Blood Indian graves near Belly River, Alberta, in the early 1880's.

Plate 2. Peigan Indians with horses and travois, 1900.

Plate 3. Sioux Indians at White Cap's camp, Saskatchewan, in 1885. White Cap is seated, centre front.

Plate 4. Sarcee Indian camp in a riverside grove near Okotoks, Alberta, 1926. The band was awaiting better weather in order to help white neighbours harvest.

Plate 5. Yellow Horse, Blackfoot head chief, and family, ca. 1910.

Plate 6. Sarcee Indians in downtown Calgary, near 7th Avenue and Centre Street, 1909. Knox Church and Hull's Opera House are in the background.

Plate 7. Mrs. Maggie Big Belly, Sarcee Indian, drying berries, ca. 1920.

Plate 8. Frank Tried To Fly and George Left Hand, Blackfoot Indians, sowing seed by hand near the North Camp, ca. 1880. Retouching is on the original print.

Plate 9. Ploughing, Stoney Reserve, Morley, Alberta, 1920's.

Plate 10. Whites and Cree Indians threshing on Crooked Lake Reserve, Saskatchewan, ca. 1900.

Plate 11. Cree grass dance, South Edmonton, 1897.

Plate 12. Horn Society dancing at Blackfoot sun dance camp, ca. 1920.

Plate 13. Sarcee Indians around sweat lodge, near Fish Creek, Sarcee Reserve, ca. 1920.

Plate 14. Blood Indians gathered outside Fort Calgary, 1878.

Plate 15. Blood Indian recruits, 191st Battalion, Fort Macleod, Alberta, 1916.
Left to right—Back: George Coming Singer (killed overseas); Joe Crow Chief; Dave Mills; George Strangling Wolf; ——. *Front*: Nick King; Harold Chief Moon; Sgt. Major Bryan; Joe and Mike Mountain Horse.

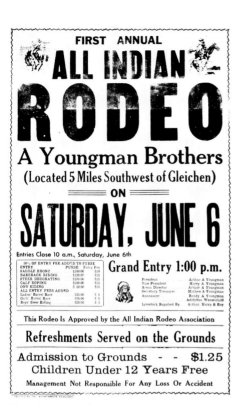

Plate 16. Poster from an all-Indian rodeo,
Blackfoot Reserve, 6 June 1964.

Plate 17. Tom Three Persons, Blood Indian
cowboy. Taken at the first Calgary
Stampede, 1912, at which he won
the world's championship for
bronco riding.

Plate 18. Bucking horse event, Banff Indian Days rodeo, 1941.

which he said, "I heard of the land question from the lips of the Reverend William Pollard in the year 1874, when he returned from visiting the Indians of Fort Simpson. In the district meeting, he declared he found the Indian greatly excited, and much dissatisfied, as white men were going in and taking up land, and the Indians claimed the land, and looked upon men who took up land as trespassers." Green further recalled that in 1877, when he took up his mission at Lakkalsap (later called Greenville), he had intended to acquire some acreage for the mission and school buildings, but he "found the idea of ownership so strong among the Indians, that I had to give the project up. I soon found that this feeling was general. Every mountain, every valley, every stream was named, and every piece belonged to some particular family."[7]

After the 1880's, the power of the missionaries in their Christian villages, such as the Roman Catholic Durieu at the Squamish reserve and the Anglican Duncan at the village of Metlakatla, had begun to decline. Missionaries in general came in for some severe criticism from settlers as a result of their part in the agitation for Indian lands. The advent of secular administration, especially in the form of Indian agents and the Indian Act, diminished missionary power and influence. Legislation to suppress the potlatch and to institute elected band councils illustrated the growing power of white control through the Department of Indian Affairs.

The breakdown of missionary power has been linked to the coming of the railroad, the influx of European settlers, and the expansion of jobs and of transportation and communication. Canneries and sawmills, lumbering and stevedoring all created new economic activities and experiences. Movement of peoples was affected. The Northwest Coast Indian tradition of travel between communities was given further impetus. English replaced Chinook jargon as the lingua franca as contacts with whites increased.

The end of the nineteenth century, when Indians were under the most intensive European impact so far experienced, saw the birth of the generation which was to give a new direction to the Indian protest. This generation partook of the religious instruction and influence which remained strong among many native communities. It also experienced more intensely than any previous generation aspects of secular white culture through Indian administration and the expanding European-dominated economic and social life.

The acceleration of white settlement and consequent pressure on the land led to a greater awareness of the necessity to act in unison on the part of Indians. Powell, writing in the 1870's, commented that it was not because of a want of grievances that the Indians had not already resorted to violent resistance to encroachment on the land, but because of a lack of unity. A number of factors were laying the foundations for a greater unity, a unity still building in the last decades of the twentieth century. The indigenous tradition of political organization based on a village unit, the multiplicity of cultural and linguistic groups, and the rivalries between groups may have contributed to attitudes of caution and resistance to participating in organizational units beyond the village or tribal levels.

Andrew Paull's career is a microcosm of the development of Indian "resurgence" or "rebirth" and the search for meaningful ways of expressing Indian identity. Shortly after his birth in 1892, Paull's parents took up permanent residence at the Squamish reserve, Mission Reserve #1, on the north shore of Burrard Inlet in what is today North Vancouver. On this reserve, years before Paull's birth, there had been established a system of government in which the missionaries of the Oblates of Mary Immaculate acted as spiritual and secular leaders of the community. Paull's family had played leadership roles in the public life of the community under this system, called the Durieu system after Bishop Paul Durieu who was its founder. Later, when Indian administration passed to federal Indian agents, the Oblates continued as pastors on the reserve. Paull's sense of purpose in later years was closely tied to the influence of the Roman Catholic Church upon him and his family. At one time he considered becoming a priest, and he received all of his formal education at the school which was established in the 1890's by the Sisters of the Child Jesus. Though not academically inclined, he early came to think of himself as having a special calling to act as a liaison between his own people and the non-Indian world. From his family, especially his grandmother, and other elders in the community, he received instruction and grounding in Squamish tradition and in public affairs. Many years later he referred to the "Indian education" he had received from tribal leaders after he had completed his "European education." He gained further knowledge of the non-Indian world from a period of work in the office of a local attorney. Through this experience, Paull developed an interest in the law as it pertained to Indians, and for much of his life he thought of himself as a kind of amateur attorney for Indians. Oral tradition surrounding Paull relates that he committed to memory long passages of laws, legal rulings, and documents related to Indian Affairs.

Paull's young manhood coincided with a period of accelerating Indian protest in British Columbia. The main issue was the Indian claim that they had an aboriginal right to the land of British Columbia which, in most of the province, had never been legally alienated. A kinsman of Paull's and chief of his own people, Chief Joe Capilano, went to England in 1906 to present a petition to King Edward VII on behalf of the Indian claim. Dissatisfaction with the Canadian government's response to the claims was clear.

Although the visit was not successful in its immediate purpose, it was part of a mounting protest by British Columbia Indians. An awareness was developing among Indians of the threat to their continued existence. By the end of the 1880's the non-Indian population had outgrown the Indian population. Between 1901 and 1911 the population of Vancouver, neighbouring the Squamish reserve, had quadrupled, reaching approximately 100,000. The Squamish became a focal point of Indian protests, even to the extent that in northern British Columbia the land protest movement was called the Capilano Movement, after one of the local Squamish bands. Other events in the southern coastal region contributed to the heightened awareness and concern over land. In both Victoria and Vancouver, Indian reserves were sold to make way for expanding cities. Negotiations and discussions over the sale of the Songhees reserve in Victoria and the Kitsilano reserve in Vancouver, in 1911 and 1913 respectively, called attention to the loss of Indian land.

In 1909, twenty tribes petitioned the King. In that year also, an organization called the Indian Tribes of the Province of British Columbia was formed. The year 1910 saw the formation of a white friends-of-the-Indians group in which two Anglican clergymen, A. E. O'Meara and L. N. Tucker, had important roles. Tucker became a prominent figure in the Anglican Church's social service concerns. In 1913 a culmination of Nishga protest over their lands led the various communities to meet together to draw up the Nishga Petition. Two years later at Spence's Bridge the Allied Tribes of British Columbia was formed.

During this period of developing events, Andrew Paull was learning about the land question through his experience in the Squamish community. The knowledge gained at his job of secretary to the local band was supplemented by wider contact with Indian peoples and issues when he was employed as an interpreter by the Royal Commission (1913–1916) set up to make final the allotment of Indian reserves. He was moving into the sphere of provincial Indian affairs, but at the same time he continued to be active at the local level and played a part in the amalgamation of the Squamish into a single band.

Paull found an outlet for his natural organizational skills in the newly formed Allied Tribes. The grass roots level of the organization was not well defined. Meetings were likely to be held only in response to crises, and delegations were chosen and funded on the basis of immediate concern. The method of protest followed the pattern of petitions and meetings with government officials established in the late nineteenth century by individual tribes or bands. Paull soon became, along with Peter Kelly, a major figure in the group. Under the influence of its lawyer, A. E. O'Meara, the Allied Tribes sought to take the land claim to the highest court of the British Empire, the Judicial

Committee of the Privy Council. O'Meara's tactic was accepted by Paull and Kelly for several years. Only toward the end of the organization's existence did the two men begin to alter their views as they gained greater knowledge of the impracticalities of this approach.

A proposal by Paull that the government give a grant to the Allied Tribes to research their claims was not accepted. Negotiations in 1923 for a settlement failed. Nevertheless, Paull and Kelly gained the respect of observers. A newspaper account of the meeting described Paull and Kelly as men of high intelligence with keen appreciation of the complexities of the issues involved.

Paull and Kelly were the main Indian spokesmen in Ottawa in 1927 when a Special Joint Committee of the Senate and House of Commons sat to consider the Allied Tribes' claims. Although records of committee discussions prior to hearing the statements of the Indians and their legal counsel show that the decision had already been reached, the presentation was listened to and questions were asked. Paull and Kelly presented the Indian interests and concerns. Paull cited various statements by public figures as well as documents and declarations of government, to support the native claim. The committee objected to this approach. Paull gave a short biographical sketch of himself. In doing so he referred to his special calling to study the Indian land question. He explained that he had emphasized oral and written sources in his study and had consulted both Indian and non-Indian sources. In addition to the larger claim to an aboriginal right to the land which had never been properly extinguished, other issues of importance to native life were also dealt with. Paull spoke about Indian fishing rights, hunting, the size of reserves, and riparian rights.

Though Paull and Kelly were complimented for their presentations, the claim to an unextinguished right to the land was denied by the committee and the hope that the committee would expedite the presentation of the claim to the Judicial Committee of the Privy Council was dashed. A special grant of $100,000 annually for the British Columbia Indians was recommended. Further pursuit of the issue was to be discouraged by making it illegal to raise money to press further the land claim. Disappointed, legal counsel O'Meara completely antagonized the committee, some of whom were predisposed to be hostile to him before the testimony was taken.

Paull's public career in native affairs was not his only interest. He had been active when a youth in sports and in his adulthood had encouraged and promoted sports among Indian youth. He occasionally wrote sports articles for the Vancouver papers and became known as a colourful character in local sports. He managed lacrosse teams and baseball teams, canoe racing, and boxing and also did some sports announcing. He promoted a sports tournament for Indian youths called the Buckskin Gloves Boxing Tournament. Dance bands, gymnastics, and beauty contests were encouraged through his activities. Paull also organized an orchestra and played several instruments. In his book, *The Fourth World*, George Manuel tells how Paull organized an employment service for Indians and speaks of him as being always engaged in organizing.

This inclination extended into the area of organizing Indian workers, and here, too, he was a leading figure. He had worked as a longshoreman and was active in the North Vancouver Longshoreman's Union. A large number of longshoremen were Indians and an Indian local, called the Bow and Arrows, was formed in the 1920's.

In the early 1940's Paull took a position of leadership in the Pacific Coast Native Fisherman's Association, a primarily Kwakiutl organization on Vancouver Island. He is credited with influencing this body to join the Native Brotherhood of British Columbia (N.B.B.C.) in 1942. The N.B.B.C. had been organized in 1930 during the Depression when the loss of employment and decline of the economy had hit the coastal fishermen very hard. When the canneries closed, fishing and canning jobs ceased. Under the leadership of a Haida, Alfred Adams, the N.B.B.C. attempted to have some impact through collective action. Like the land question, the economic conditions stimulated united action by large groups of native people. The N.B.B.C., though begun as an organization of northern coastal Indians, spread its influence southward due to the work of Andrew Paull. Following the amalgamation of 1942, Paull was appointed business manager for the N.B.B.C. He held this position for about two years but resigned over disputes regarding the scope and powers of the job. The office had not been clearly defined and some objections were raised to Paull's handling of it. In this role as earlier, Paull attempted to encourage contact and co-operation between Indians and non-governmental groups and organizations. Particularly he was interested in making available to Indians resources outside of those of Indian Affairs.

Paull's horizons continued to spread. He moved from a smaller to a larger field of action. He conceived of a native organization on a national or even international level. The result was the North American Indian Brotherhood (N.A.I.B.), formed in June 1944 at a meeting in Ottawa. Paull became president of the N.A.I.B. in September 1945.

The N.A.I.B. immediately took up a watch-dog role in Indian affairs. Conventions were held in Ottawa to be nearer federal offices. Paull saw it as a kind of Indian commonwealth of nations. He denied any religious bias or backing. Critics questioned the existence of a strong grass roots constituency for the N.A.I.B. The president, Paull, and the executive were said by some to be "all head and no tail." Paull drew prominent figures from across the country into the organization, but efforts to draw in provincial organizations between 1945 and 1950 were unsuccessful. Paull had hoped to build a complex of organizations on the basis of local, provincial, and national (N.A.I.B.) links.

Post-war developments in Canada led the government to re-examine the Indian administration. A parliamentary committee sat to receive presentations from Indians and non-Indians. Paull appeared before and made representations to the committee several times. In 1946 he urged rethinking of Indian status. He raised the issue of citizenship and wardship. He referred to failures of government to abide by treaty terms and mismanagement within Indian administration, and called for the appointment of more Indians to top posts in Indian administration and for self-government on reserves. Contrary to the stance of some Indian organizations, Paull called for the continuation of government-supported denominational schools for Indians. He asserted that the N.A.I.B. had been instrumental in bringing about the parliamentary committee.

In his 1947 address to the committee, he called attention to particular concerns of British Columbia such as the still unresolved land claim. Again, as in 1927, he asserted that Indian land had never been legally acquired. He spoke of Indian concerns about irrigation, grazing lands, trapping, and improved transportation facilities for reserves.

The last decade of his life was one of growing feebleness as a result of illness and failing eyesight. Nevertheless, until his death in 1959 Paull continued to be active at various levels on behalf of Indians. Whether at the local or provincial level or on a national policy level, Paull acted as a constant irritant to the Indian administration. He was not willing to see Indians assimilated, though he did not have a foolproof plan to prevent it.

He was groping for a compromise which would allow Indians to retain their identity and continue to grow and develop as individuals, and as a people within Canada and North America. In the process of doing this, he was sometimes thought of as eccentric or even retrograde. Throughout his public life his actions and his public statements were controversial.

It is part of the significance of Paull's career that he was personally involved in so many of the economic and social activities in which Indians interacted with non-Indians during this period in the fields of employment and labour organizations, Indian organization and protest, legal matters, reserve life, and reserve public affairs. Being active in so many areas, Paull resembled in some ways the early missionaries with their diverse activities. In his public life, Paull followed much of the pattern already set in Indian protest. He wrote letters on behalf of individuals and groups to various levels of government and to the newspapers. He spoke in public, employing a dramatic and flamboyant style. From participation at the local level, his public career expanded to the provincial level and beyond, as his involvement in Indian concerns increased.

The formation of the Allied Tribes was a step in the development of a larger Indian identity. Groupings based on units larger than the aboriginal units helped to create new levels of common action. The issue of the land claim, augmented by others such as education, social services, and discrimination, contributed to nationwide Indian identity and organization. The same or related issues have contributed to the creation of a larger Indian identity beyond Canada's borders. Paull was sensitive to these issues, and his career was a response to them. He envisioned and attempted to implement the vision of an expanding Indian unity and co-operation into an international brotherhood. He was a precursor of present-day protest in that he was involved in a variety of areas of Indian concern and tried to deal with them in ways which allowed for the retention of Indian culture without attempting to turn back the clock by withdrawing from the dominant society. His career illustrates both continuity and change. Because he did not present a systematic formula for dealing with each issue, he sometimes appeared to be taking contradictory stances from one time to the next and from one issue to another. He was both an innovator and a conservator.

Paull's career overlaps all four of the phases of the Van Dyke–Sanders system, and yet it does not fit exactly. Paull was feeling his way. He took a pragmatic approach to issues. He was not a transitional figure in the sense of being in between traditional and assimilated roles. Nor does he fit neatly into a conservative-progressive dichotomy, though he was regarded by some of his Indian contemporaries as conservative, perhaps even eccentrically conservative.

His career comes after the decline of the theocratic era in Indian history in various parts of British Columbia. Durieu and Duncan and the others had been replaced by Indian administration. Where the missionary or white pastor remained, his status had changed: he was much more of an adviser than a commander. As an adviser, he was no longer an intermediary, since the Indians had come to take an active part in their own affairs. As they gained greater expertise in the workings of Euro-Canadian society, men like Paull and Kelly were more effective without the aid of their advisers.

From the 1880's to the 1920's, the Indians in British Columbia took over the organizational control of their protest movement. The period of the 1930's to the 1960's saw an acceleration of this trend. The development of native expertise and the elaboration of native issues into not only a provincial and national context, but also an international context, have taken place in the 1970's. In the development of Indian responsibility for their own affairs, Andrew Paull exerted a constant and lasting influence.

Notes

[1]Elizabeth Van Dyke and Douglas Sanders, "A History of British Columbia Indian Political Organizations." Manuscript in the author's possession. Editors' note: For a more detailed analysis of Andrew Paull's career, see E. Palmer Patterson II, "Andrew Paull and Canadian Indian Resurgence" (Ph.D. diss., University of Washington, 1963).

[2]Indian Chiefs of Alberta, *Citizens Plus* (Indian Association of Alberta, 1970).

[3]See Robin Fisher, *Contact and Conflict: Indian-European Relations in British Columbia, 1774-1890* (Vancouver: University of British Columbia Press, 1977), pp. 162-72.

[4]See Robert E. Cail, *Land, Man, and the Law: The Disposal of Crown Lands in British Columbia, 1871-1913* (Vancouver: University of British Columbia Press, 1974), pp. 169-243.

[5]The controversy at Metlakatla has been more extensively analyzed than any other aspect of Protestant missions in British Columbia. The most recent study, by Jean Usher, *William Duncan of Metlakatla* (Ottawa: National Museums of Canada, 1978) is the most useful.

[6]Letters from the Methodist Missionary Society to the Superintendent-General of Indian Affairs respecting the British Columbia troubles, with affidavits and declarations, in British Columbia Archives Library, Victoria, nos. 56 and 57.

[7]Ibid., no. 14.

6

Displaced Red Men
The Sioux in Canada

GEORGE F. G. STANLEY

I

Indian-white relations in Canada have been influenced by many Indians who fled to Canada from south of the border to escape retaliation or annihilation at the hands of the Americans. The Abenaki, Caughnawaga,[1] Delaware, and Mohawk Indians of central Canada are some examples. In several instances these Indians fought alongside the Canadians in the wars against the Americans during the eighteenth and nineteenth centuries. For their services they received land grants or "reserves" in what are now the provinces of Quebec and Ontario, at St. François, Sault St. Louis, St. Regis, Deseronto, and Grand River. These grants did not imply a formal recognition on the part of the French or British authorities of any legal aboriginal title to the lands under Canadian jurisdiction. They were simply reserves of grace, the gifts of a benevolent French king and a grateful British monarch.[2]

Still another group of Indians who may be classified as refugee Indians in Canada were the members of the Sioux nation who fled to the Red River and the North West Territories during the second half of the nineteenth century. The Sioux (or Dakota) formed a loose kind of confederacy of seven council fires.[3] It included the *Mdewakantonwan*, or "Spirit Lake People"; *Wahpekute*, or "Shooters among the Leaves"; *Sisitonwan*, or "People of the Ridged Fish Scales"; *Wahpetonwan*, or "Dwellers among the Leaves"; *Thanktonwan*, or "Dwellers at the End"; *Thanktonwana*, or "Little Dwellers at the End"; *Titonwan*, or "Dwellers on the Plains." They are said to have originated in the wooded country south and west of Lake Superior, a region they occupied, despite the withdrawal of the Assiniboine to the north into what is now Western Canada,[4] until they first came into contact with the white man. Their economy was based upon hunting, fishing, harvesting wild rice, and gardening.[5] It was with good reason that the Jesuit,

Jacques Marquette, referred to them, in 1669, as the Iroquois of the north-west.[6]

The position held by the Sioux on the upper Mississippi did not go un-challenged. The continental spread of the Algonkian-speaking Indians, retiring before the onslaught of the eastern Iroquois, brought them into conflict with the Ojibwa (Chippewa), which resulted in a long, drawn-out war with the Sioux that lasted into the nineteenth century. Yielding to the pressure of their antagonists, the Sioux withdrew slowly westwards along the Minnesota river and even to the Missouri. Finally, in 1825 the Ojibwa–Sioux war came to an end when the American authorities were able to per-suade the contending parties to come together at Prairie du Chien and to agree upon a common boundary line between them.[7]

The withdrawal of the Sioux from the country of the upper Mississippi placed them on the edge of the great plains. Although originally a woodland people, the Sioux adapted easily to the new geographical scene and to a new economy. This was owing largely to the fact that the horse had made its way into the Minnesota country in the early part of the eighteenth century.[8] The Sioux became renowned as the most accomplished horsemen and buffalo hunters of the Prairies.

As settlement patterns finally stabilized, the Sioux nation formed three well-defined groups. The first four divisions mentioned previously became associated together as the Santee; the fifth and sixth as the Yankton; and the last as the Teton. Each group developed its own internal subdivisions, and they occupied, respectively, southern Minnesota, eastern South Dakota, and western South Dakota and parts of Montana and Wyoming.

French fur traders began to push westwards in the late seventeenth century, by-passing the intermediate Indian nations to deal directly with those tribes, such as the Sioux, who had access to new and undepleted fur reserves. This policy, however, irritated the Indian middlemen, the Fox among them, who resented the loss of their profits and disliked the idea of their rivals acquiring "firesticks" from the French.

The French wanted to keep the peace with all Indian nations and bent their diplomatic efforts to that end. But they were not always able to reconcile competing Indian interests. In fact their whole western Indian policy seemed to fall apart during the early years of the eighteenth century. Trade dried up in the face of the active hostility of the Fox and the veiled hostility of the Sioux, who had killed La Vérendrye's son, Jean, the missionary Fr. Aulneau, and nineteen Canadian *voyageurs* on an island in Lake of the Woods in 1736 when they felt the French were becoming too friendly with their traditional rivals, the Ojibwa. Even though in 1740 Paul Marin persuaded delegates from several Western Indian nations to accompany him to Montreal to make humble and conciliatory speeches to the Canadian governor general, French sovereignty in the Western lands remained precarious. During the final struggle with the Anglo-Americans during the Seven Years' War, the French called for and did obtain some help from Western tribes, including the Sioux; but this assistance was only of a limited nature—not of sufficient strength to forestall the fall of Montreal in 1760. Three years later when France surrendered all of its claims to the northern half of North America, it left inter-tribal warfare as well as the Indian trade as its legacy to Great Britain.

In the Proclamation of 1763 the British defined the boundary between the Indian territory and the settled colonies of America by drawing a line from Fort Stanwix along the crest of the Allegheny mountains. Beyond this line, to the west, was the country of the Indians. The British saw this territory as a means of controlling both the Indians and the Indian trade; the Americans saw it as a British scheme to limit American trade and territorial expansion. The British clung to this idea of a Western Indian state until the conclusion of the War of 1812; the Americans, however, wanted all land to the Mississippi for their own exploding population. Consequently, the Western Indians, including the Sioux, were disposed to look with more favour upon the British cause than upon the American cause during the American Revolutionary War and the War of 1812.[9]

The outbreak of war between Great Britain and the United States in June 1812 demonstrated the extent to which the Indians were committed to Great Britain. Anticipating trouble, Robert Dickson,[10] the British fur trader, rushed to the West to raise a corps of Indian warriors in the British interest. He went as far as the Sioux country, where he approached the Santee chiefs, Wabasha and Little Crow. Both responded favourably. Little Crow recalled the "generous conduct" of the British in the past and promised his full support. So, too, did Wabasha.[11] Hence we find the Sioux participating in the British capture of Michilimackinac in July 1812;[12] in the British operations in August 1812, leading to the capture of Detroit;[13] in the attack on Fort Meigs in 1813;[14] and in the capture of Prairie du Chien on the upper Mississippi in 1814.[15]

II

The years which followed the War of 1812 were not happy years for the Indian people. They were years of declining numbers, of wars, pestilence, and diminishing food resources. They were years in which the Indians entered into a series of so-called treaties with the United States, only to discover that these agreements were designed less to assist the Indians to contend with the expansion of white settlement than to divert the Indian trade from the British traders to the Americans. Some American romantics spent these years deploring the decline in the numbers of the Indians and speaking and writing about the "vanishing red man"; but most Americans seemed anxious to speed him on his way. Andrew Jackson probably expressed the American grass roots approach to Indians during these years when he declared that Indian land rights were a fiction and that it was "high time to do away with the farce of treating with Indian tribes."[16] Not surprisingly, it was during Jackson's tenure of office as president of the United States that Congress adopted the Indian Removal Act of 1830, by which all Indians were to be removed from east of the Mississippi and settled west of that river in a new Indian territory from which, with the exception of a few government officials and soldiers, all whites would be excluded.[17]

Some of the Indians went willingly. Others went at the point of the bayonet. But all went. Cherokee, Choctaw, and others from the south; Shawnee, Ojibwa, Sac, Fox, and others from the north. Finally, in 1871, the ultimate in Jacksonian Indian policy was achieved, when the United States declared, "hereafter, no Indian nation or tribe within the territory of the United States shall be acknowledged or recognized as an independent tribe or power .with whom the United States may contract by treaty."[18] In other words, Indians were not to be regarded as independent nations; they were, instead, to be looked upon as domestic, dependent communities occupying their own territories.

The most significant of the so-called treaties entered into (one cannot properly use the word "negotiated," since there was virtually no Indian input) by the Sioux were those of 1851,[19] by which the Santee surrendered some 24 million acres of land in return for a reserve ten miles wide on each side of the Minnesota river between Lake Traverse and Yellow Medicine River, a distance of about 160 kilometres, and a monetary payment of $1,665,000 of which $1,360,000 were to be set up as a trust fund. Thus, 1851 marks, as far as the Santee were concerned, the triumph of the white man's manifest destiny, the opening up of the American West. But this triumph was achieved only at the expense of Indian goodwill. The smouldering resentments engendered by the treaties of 1851 burst into flame as white settlers poured into Minnesota. They came in such numbers that the one-time village with the Santee–Greek name, Minneapolis, aspired to city status.

The Indians were not all of one mind about the arrangement of 1851. There were those, the "cut-hair and breeches" Indians, who tried seriously to follow the white man's road to industry, cleanliness, monogamy, and sabbath-keeping; there were others, the "scalp-lock and blanket" Indians, who wanted to live in the old ways. The principal Santee chief, Little Crow, a grandson of the Indian of the same name who had fought for the British in the War of 1812, tried to straddle the fence. He invited Christian missionaries to come to his reserve and himself attended church; at the same time he kept his six wives and their twenty-two children.[20] He did not like the treaty of 1851; still he appended his name to it, along with Wabasha, another Santee chief bearing a name familiar in British military history.

The new settlers were not, however, interested in the Sioux until suddenly, in August 1862, several Santee, returning from a hunting expedition, killed a few whites as well as deer. Little Crow was alarmed. He knew what the American response would be. He therefore advised caution. But Little Crow's counsel failed to cool the hotheads, and in order to prove that he was no coward, he took over the leadership of the war party.[21] The Sioux outbreak may have been a spontaneous action, or it may have been a carefully planned eruption. Regardless, what is important is the basic cause, and that was the white man's hunger, his hunger for land, his schemes for railways, industry, and state-making. Henry Whipple, the Episcopalian bishop, blamed it on Washington's Indian policy, with its pauperizing annuities, its political appointments, its small reserves, and its deliberate attempt to break down the economy and social organization of the Indian tribes.[22] Other contemporaries offered as additional factors the warlike tradition of the Sioux and the absence of many of the white settlers off to fight for the freedom of the negroes.

The Sioux War of 1862–63 could, of course, have only one end. After a brief initial success, the Indians were defeated. Some fled to join the Yankton and Teton on the Missouri river; others made their way towards the British territory to the north. Those who did not leave huddled in camps around Fort Snelling. Some 392 Indians were tried for murder: 303 of them were sentenced to death. Thirty-eight sang their death song before their execution. The remaining Santee in Minnesota were transported beyond its boundaries. The Ojibwa, the traditional enemies of the Sioux, surrendered their lands and withdrew to the northern woodlands. The Winnebago, a small and harmless band, fled to Dakota. Minnesotans wanted no more Indians among them after the events of 1862.[23]

The fighting which began in 1862 did not end with the hangings or with the death of Little Crow.[24] It simply spread to the West. For several years, under Red Cloud and Spotted Tail, the Teton continued to fight the battle the Santee had started. Finally, in 1868, all fighting came to an end and peace terms were agreed upon. "From this day forward, all war among the parties to this agreement shall forever cease": that was the stipulation to which Red Cloud agreed.[25] "No white person or persons shall be permitted to settle upon or occupy any portion of the territory [that is, the Black Hills, the land of the Teton Sioux] or without the consent of the Indian to pass through the same": that was the stipulation to which General Sherman affixed his signature.[26] The Indians might have kept their part of the bargain; the white men did not keep theirs.

When the treaty of Laramie was drafted in 1868, the Black Hills of Dakota were considered worthless by the American authorities. But when the rumours of gold in the Hills reached the outside world, men ignored the Indian boundary lines and rushed to dig the precious yellow metal. When the Indians tried to stop the miners and the prospectors, American troops were sent to protect them. Nobody, except the Teton, seemed to remember that the trespassers were supposed to obtain the permission of the Indians. President Grant had previously made a show of his determination to prevent all "invasion" of the Sioux country by "intruders," so "long as by law and treaty" the land was "secured to the Indians."[27] But in the end what could Grant do but protect his own people? Red Cloud and Spotted Tail, now both good agency Indians, protested. Forced to act, the American government decided to buy out the Indian rights in the Black Hills, and sent commissioners to negotiate a sale. In view of the significance of the Hills to the Sioux, the proposal and the action were both impractical. Money could not buy the region, and the disconcerted commissioners returned to Washington with the recommendation that the American government expropriate the area. Considering the determined stand taken by the Sioux, expropriation was tantamount to a declaration of war. What the commissioners did not antici-pate was that it would be a war which would lead to the worst humiliation ever suffered by American troops in all their Indian wars, the annihilation of George Custer's 7th Cavalry at the Little Big Horn in 1876. But Sitting Bull, Gall, and Crazy Horse were no more able to resist the full military power of the United States than Little Crow had been. In the end the Teton were compelled to make peace. Those who would not, like Sitting Bull, fled north to British territory.

III

The Sioux were no strangers to the country north of the 49th parallel.[28] Not only had they engaged in scuffles with the Saulteaux (the name given to the Ojibwa who migrated onto the Canadian Plains), but they also had, from time to time, engaged the Red River métis on the plains while hunting the buffalo. It was indeed partly as a defence measure against the Sioux that the métis devised their semi-military organization while on the plains, which was, both in 1869–70 and in 1885, the main source of Louis Riel's strength. Sometimes the encounters between the Sioux and the métis involved no more than an exchange of musket shots; sometimes they involved full scale battles, such as that which took place at the Grand Coteau in 1851.[29] But there had never been any long or bitter wars between the Sioux and the métis, even when the Saulteaux joined forces with the métis on the Prairies. Any fears of a war with the Sioux were allayed by the despatch of British troops to Red River, and when a large band of Sioux visited Fort Garry in 1860 there was no hint of any ill feeling.[30] This visit was followed by a pledge of amity in 1861.[31] It was a recognition of their lack of hostility towards the British that the Santee studiously avoided any threat to the Hudson's Bay post at Georgetown during the rising of 1862–63.

The first Sioux refugees appeared in Red River as early as December 1862. They were furnished with rations by the governor of Rupert's Land, A. G. Dallas, and encouraged to leave for the plains. The people of Red River suspected, however, that they were but the vanguard of a much larger refugee army to follow. To bolster defence, Dallas and the Council of Assiniboia asked the Queen to send her troops back to Fort Garry. A military force might be needed to cope with a large-scale migration of Santee warriors across the frontier.[32] London agreed to provide troops if the Hudson's Bay Company would pay all expenses, including the pay and allowances of the troops, their rations, and their transportation. Dallas therefore limited his preparations to informing post managers to refrain from supplying the Indians with ammunition.

In the spring of 1863 the Sioux came in greater numbers. In May, Little Crow himself arrived at Fort Garry to remind Dallas that the Sioux were one-time allies of the Crown and that his grandfather had served during the War of 1812. Little Crow wanted provisions and ammunition. Dallas could give him the first, but could not provide the second; he did, however, promise to intercede with the American military authorities on behalf of the Indians. The subsequent death of Little Crow accelerated the movement of Santee refugees across the frontier. On 11 December, Dallas wrote to London informing his superiors that he was now looking after some 445 Sioux Indians, men, women and children, all of them "in a state of positive starvation." They had no food, no ammunition, no clothes.[33] They were even prepared to offer their children for sale for a little sustenance.[34] The situation was so appalling that Dallas was willing to risk the enmity of the Americans by providing the Indians with a little ammunition, as well as food and fishing tackle, on the undertaking that they would use it "only to hunt game."

Because they did not want to face the winter on the plains without warmer clothing and a few supplies, the Sioux, now numbering six hundred, were inclined to remain around Fort Garry. Some settlers wanted to compel them to leave. But Dallas weighed the pros and cons of using force, and informed the company's head office "It will, I believe, cost us less to maintain all these Sioux for ten years than to go to war with them."[35] He was right. In the end, persuasion and pemmican did get the Indians to move, some to Lake Manitoba, some to the White Horse Plains. A few of them even went back to the United States, where an ex-Indian agent turned cavalry man, Edwin Hatch, was waiting to receive them at Pembina.

The inhabitants of Red River, whites and métis alike, were frightened by the presence of so many destitute Santee in British territory. They wanted them out of the country and even talked about inviting Hatch into the settlement to drive the Indians back across the frontier at sabre point. While Dallas temporized, several local people took matters into their own hands. They plied Little Six (Little Crow's half-brother) and Medicine Bottle with liquor, and then, when the two chiefs were drunk, drugged them with laudanum and chloroform, bound them, and carried them off to a grateful Major Hatch.[36] This "gross violation of International Law," as the *Canadian News* called it,[37] led to arched eyebrows in London, but not to diplomatic protests. Nothing was done while the major removed his prisoners to Fort Snelling, where they were subsequently tried on charges of murder and executed in November 1865.[38] Dallas was alarmed at the thought of what might follow from the kidnapping and annoyed at the constant demands of those Red River inhabitants who wanted Hatch to come into the settlement and finish the job. Finally Dallas yielded to public pressure and informed Hatch that he and his men were free to cross the frontier. He stipulated only that they should "take such measures as will prevent bloodshed or violence in the houses or inclosures of the settlers, should any of the Sioux Indians take refuge there."[39] Interestingly enough, Hatch did not take advantage of this permission. After a winter at Pembina his men were in no condition to undertake "active operations" and most of his horses had perished. Instead of going north to Fort Garry, Hatch was content to go south to Fort Abercrombie.[40]

The Santee Sioux departed for the plains for the spring hunt in 1864, but in August another group, numbering nearly three thousand Indians, arrived at Fort Garry. These Sioux were Sisseton who had held aloof from the fighting in Minnesota, but who had been pursued by the American troops to whom any Sioux was an enemy. Defeated at Big Mound, the Indians had spent the winter not far from the international frontier, and then they had moved north into British territory, led by Standing Buffalo, Waanatan, the Leaf, and Turning Thunder. They had already written to Dallas, only to receive his advice to "make peace with the Americans, who have assured me they are willing to be friends with all the Sioux who have not actually committed murder."[41] But instead of making peace with the Americans, they arrived at an understanding with the Canadian Saulteaux and Cree, and in August landed on Dallas's doorstep. Like the Santee who had come with Little Crow and Little Six, Standing Buffalo's followers were destitute. Like Little Crow's men they brought their old British medals with them and their recollections of the promises the British had made to them during the War of 1812. Like their predecessors they asked for assistance. And like them, too, committed no depredations, at least not at the outset. However, when the governor of Assiniboia refused them assistance, they helped themselves to local livestock, corn, and potatoes. Some visited the homes of the whites who had cared for the Sioux children during the winter and demanded their return.[42] Then they moved westwards to the buffalo plains.

During the next two years, Standing Buffalo's Indians followed the seasonal migrations of the buffalo, scrupulously avoiding any encounters with the whites. In 1869 Standing Buffalo died of wounds received in a shooting fray with some Crow Indians. Lacking his leadership, the band began to disintegrate. A number of Indians had already drifted back to the United States; others had settled at Devil's Lake. Others joined the Santee bands still hunting in the Qu'Appelle region. One small group under White Eagle moved to Wood Mountain, and was there when the first Teton refugees arrived in the autumn of 1876.[43]

The movement of the Sioux to British territory in 1876 and 1877 did not follow the same pattern as that of 1862 and 1863. In the earlier period the British West had been under the control of the Hudson's Bay Company; in 1876–77 it was part of the Canadian Confederation. In the earlier period there was no armed force available to assist the authorities; in the later period the Indians had to deal with the recently formed North West Mounted Police. The one thing common to both periods was the fact that the Sioux displayed their British medals and recalled to the minds of the British authorities the services they had rendered the Crown between 1812 and 1814.

The first Teton to reach Canada was Black Moon, who arrived with forty-two lodges in the autumn of 1876. Before the end of the year nearly three thousand men, women and children, and thirty-five hundred horses were encamped in the region of the Cypress Hills and Wood Mountain.[44] Then, in May 1877, came Four Horns and Sitting Bull, with the remnants of the army which had fought at the Little Big Horn. The concentration of so many fighting Sioux in southern Saskatchewan, close by the American frontier, raised many questions for Canada. Would the Sioux refrain from carrying out attacks on the Americans from a safe base on the Canadian side? Would the Saulteaux, Cree, and Blackfoot remain quiet when confronted with the added pressures the Sioux would exert upon the dwindling herds of buffalo? The possibilities of trouble in the Canadian North West were frightening.

It was fortunate for Canada that the men who met and talked with the Teton refugees were policemen whose straightforward approach won Sioux goodwill. Superintendent James Morrow Walsh told Four Horns—and it was the same thing he had told Black Moon and would tell Sitting Bull— that if the Sioux refrained from killing or injuring Canadian settlers, from stealing their goods or horses, or bearing false witness, they would be allowed to remain on Canadian soil. What was more, they could sleep soundly in their tipis, and rely upon the red-coated police to protect them.[45]

However soundly the Sioux might sleep in the Cypress Hills, the politicians and civil servants in Ottawa were afraid of what the Canadian Indians might do, and, even more, what the Americans might do. Even before the battle of the Little Big Horn, the Canadian governor general, Lord Dufferin, had written to the colonial secretary in London, expressing his concern lest Canada be "placed in great difficulties should the Indians with whom the Yankees are at war, be driven into our territories and attempt to make them the base of their operations against their pursuers."[46]

For the moment there appeared to be no danger. Sitting Bull told the police that he "had buried his arms on the American side of the line" before crossing into Canada,[47] and Walsh, to alleviate their hunger, had permitted the Indians to purchase a small amount of ammunition for hunting. On 30 May, the chief commissioner of the N.W.M.P., James Macleod, wrote to Ottawa suggesting that an approach might be made to Washington "to ascertain upon what terms" the Americans would take the Sioux back into the United States. "I fancy that they would only be too glad to have them return," he wrote.[48] Macleod over-estimated the Americans' response to the return of Sitting Bull, but he did make his point with Prime Minister Alexander Mackenzie, who was particularly concerned lest the appearance of the Sioux within the boundaries of Western Canada discourage white settlers from migrating to that part of the country.

Not surprisingly, within a month of Sitting Bull's arrival, the British minister at Washington, Sir Francis Plunkett, took up the question of the Sioux with the State Department. The Americans, less interested in the Sioux than Macleod had hoped, were inclined to temporize; or perhaps it was simply that the secretary of state, William Evarts, was never anything more than a diplomatic dabbler.[49] The Sioux, he replied, were political offenders seeking asylum in a foreign land, and the United States had, therefore, neither the right to demand their extradition nor the authority to cross the Canadian frontier to remove them by force. Canada was welcome to keep them. But if the State Department could thus casually dismiss the Sioux question, the American military could not. They were outspoken about the presence of the Sioux on the frontier. According to General Sherman, it was Canada's neighbourly duty to round up those "bloody savages" and compel them to return to the United States; and to assist the Canadians, Americans were ready to expedite the shipment of ammunition for the use of the Mounted Police from Eastern Canada to Western Canada through American territory.[50] The feeling among the military was that, if the Canadians were unwilling to do their duty by the United States, the Americans should do the job themselves. Just to complicate matters there were those semi-official emissaries, private meddlers like the Catholic priest who came to Canada bearing letters from the Office of Indian Affairs in Washington, ostensibly to persuade the Sioux to return home, but in actual fact to urge them to stay in Canada, where they were bound to be better off. Small wonder Canadians were sometimes perplexed by the apparent contradictions in American Indian policy. In any event, nothing would move Sitting Bull. He told the Mounted

Police that he had come to Canada "to remain with the White Mother's children."[51]

Ottawa did not want to keep the Sioux. Far removed from the impact of Sitting Bull's personality, the politicians in Canada's capital were never as impressed by the Sioux chief as were Irvine and Walsh. To Ottawa he was a nuisance or, what was worse, an embarrassment. Canada was just in the midst of arranging treaties with the Western Indians, including the Cree and Blackfoot, and did not want the waters of Indian diplomacy muddied by the Sioux. Prime Minister Alexander Mackenzie hurriedly sent his minister of the interior, David Mills, to Washington to urge the president of the United States to take another look at the Sioux question. Mackenzie's action was without precedent, a serious departure from established diplomatic practice of a colony operating through the British Foreign Office. Canada's breach of diplomatic etiquette could well prove a dangerous precedent.[52] Mackenzie's principal argument was the urgency of the matter.[53] He could also have argued that Mills achieved what Mackenzie wanted. Did not the Americans agree to reconsider the question and to appoint a commission to go to Canada to talk with Sitting Bull?

The composition of the commission was not such as to promise success: A. H. Terry, who had commanded the American troops in the 1876 Dakota campaign, and A. G. Lawrence, who had been a member of the 1875 force which had deprived the Sioux of the Black Hills. The commissioners were authorized to offer the Sioux a full pardon, but only on condition that they surrender all their guns and their horses. To help the commission, the Mounted Police were requested by Ottawa to assist the negotiations in every way, "persuasive" but not "compulsory."[54] The *National Republican* probably spoke the truth when it stated "it would be pleasing to this government if the proposition did not succeed, as Sitting Bull is not a denizen to be desired by any country."[55]

At first, Sitting Bull would not even meet with the commissioners. However, assured by Walsh that Canada had no desire to compel him to accept any American offer, he agreed to listen, but adamantly refused to negotiate with the Americans. He flatly rejected their terms, replying "This part of the country does not belong to your people. You belong on the other side. This side belongs to us."[56]

The American government was content with the failure of the commission; the Canadian government was not. And the winter of 1877–78 only added to Ottawa's worries. There were no buffalo to be found in southern Saskatchewan and the Sioux grew restive as they grew hungry. To all Indians the buffalo was the source of life; and with métis, Canadian Indians, and American refugees competing for the few remaining animals, all were compelled to risk sending hunting parties to the United States. Inevitably, such hunting parties lead to rumours of a vast Indian conspiracy to overrun the whole

American North West. It was nonsense, of course; but nonsense all too frequently finds eager believers and willing propagandists. Not that Alexander Mackenzie believed the conspiracy story, nor did his successor in office, Sir John A. Macdonald. But Canadians generally could not rid themselves of the feeling that the presence of the Sioux was not in the best interests of the country.[57] They posed a threat to "peace" because American military men were always talking about the dangers of an Indian war, and Evarts was constantly demanding to know why the Mounted Police had not interned the Sioux and why the Indians were permitted to purchase ammunition.[58] Evarts was a bore. General Nelson Miles was a menace with his charges that the North West Mounted Police were providing Sitting Bull with arms in the hope of prodding the Indians into warlike actions against the United States.[59]

It says much for the cool-headed approach of the N.W.M.P. that nothing untoward happened and that Walsh kept on speaking to General Miles, urging him to modify the demand that the Sioux give up their arms and their horses. "If this could be arranged, they will probably give up," he told Miles. "This will start with thirty or forty families crossing over and the others waiting to hear of their reception and treatment. Detachment by detachment they will all go; Bull will be the last."[60]

Time proved that Walsh was right. A trickle of Indians towards the United States did start, not because Miles modified the American terms, but because the Americans were in a position to offer food to starving Indians. Partly, too, because the Canadian authorities suspected that Walsh's policy of befriending Sitting Bull encouraged the old chief and the Teton to remain in Canada. Walsh was therefore posted elsewhere, and the officer who followed him, L. N. F. Crozier, ignored Bull and concentrated on helping the Indians break away from his control and move from Canadian territory. They left in small groups just as Walsh had said they would, and by May 1880, only five hundred of the four thousand who came to Canada still remained.[61] Even Sitting Bull went in the end, although not until his last appeal for a reserve in Canada had been rejected by the unsympathetic Indian commissioner, Edgar Dewdney, and the old chief was reduced to eating roots and gophers.[62] After four years of refuge in Canada, his spirit was broken.

IV

After the Hudson's Bay Company surrendered its territorial jurisdiction to Canada in July 1870, it was imperative that steps be taken to clear away the impediments to massive immigration imposed by aboriginal Indian ownership rights.[63] Accordingly, the federal government of Canada appointed special commissioners to arrange with the Indians for the surrender of their rights. Between 1871 and 1877, seven treaties were concluded with the Cree, Saulteaux, Assiniboine, Blackfoot, Peigan, Blood, Sarcee, and Stoney Indians, by which Canada acquired full rights in the greater part of the habitable region between Lake of the Woods and the Rocky Mountains. There was not much in the way of negotiation. The Indian Department decided what it was prepared to offer and expected the Indians to accept the terms proposed. In return for the surrender by the Indians of "all their right and title" to the area in question, the Canadian government promised to provide the Indians with fixed annuities; specially reserved areas for their homes which could not be alienated without their own consent; agricultural implements, seed grain, oxen, and cattle. At the request of the Indians themselves, alcohol was to be banned from the reserves. In several ways the Canadian treaties differed from those in effect south of the border. In Canada the reserves were much smaller than those in the United States. Canada's policy was to provide reserves for Indian bands, rather than for Indian nations. The reasoning behind this policy was that small reserves, scattered throughout areas of white settlement, would provide the Indians with ready markets for their produce; at the same time they would provide the white settlers with a ready source of labour.[64]

The Sioux, of course, were not included in the Canadian treaties.[65] These Indians appreciated the fact that they had no aboriginal rights in the area surrendered. Still, they were anxious for reserves of their own on which they might eventually settle down. Requests were therefore forwarded to the lieutenant-governor of Manitoba. The lieutenant-governor, A. G. Archibald, was sympathetic, and his successor, Alexander Morris, wrote to Ottawa both in 1872 and 1873, urging that a favourable response be given to the Sioux petition.[66] For once Ottawa acted reasonably promptly. On 14 January 1874, an order-in-council authorized the granting of 12,000 acres to the refugee Sioux. The first site chosen for a reserve was rejected by the Indians, owing to the absence of adequate supplies of wood. Moreover, the Indians preferred to have two small reserves rather than one larger one. New sites were selected in 1875; one, of 7,936 acres, on the Assiniboine at Oak river, and the other, of 6,885 acres, farther west at Bird Tail Creek, near Fort Ellice. The size of the reserve in each instance was determined by the formula of allotting eighty acres to each family of five.[67]

There were still a number of Sioux who showed little interest in settling down. Some of these Indians camped near Portage la Prairie, where they had been able to find intermittent employment with white farmers; others were roving the country about Turtle Mountain in search of buffalo. Two more bands were located in the vicinity of the Qu'Appelle Lakes. The Portage group was not provided with a reserve until 1898.[68] The Turtle Mountain Sioux were allotted a reserved area in 1877, along Pipestone Creek near Oak Lake.[69] The few determined souls who would not move to Oak Lake were finally given a minuscule reserve, one mile square, on the north slope of Turtle Mountain.[70] The bands led by Standing Buffalo (a son of the former chief of the same name) and White Cap still believed that they could live by the hunt. White Cap told a representative of the Department of Indian Affairs in 1875 that he and his followers had lived in Canada for thirteen years, had given the authorities no trouble and desired to be "left as they were, and have the privilege of hunting with the half-breeds of the Qu'Appelle Lakes."[71] Several years later, when the question of a reserve was raised once again, Standing Buffalo was given a reserve on the Qu'Appelle Lakes, and White Cap, who was then living near Batoche, was provided with a reserve at Moose Woods on the South Saskatchewan river.[72] Subsequently, in 1894, a small band of Wahpeton Sioux received a reserve near Prince Albert.

While the Canadian government was carrying on its plans to settle the refugees from the Sioux War in Minnesota on its reserves, it was, at the same time, refusing to do the same thing for the refugees from the Sioux Wars in Dakota. This apparent inconsistency derived from the arrival of the Minnesota Sioux on the Canadian Prairies prior to the acquisition of that region by Canada, thus establishing a claim to preferred treatment. The Teton bands arrived after Canada had established her sovereignty, and the great majority of them were eventually persuaded to return to the United States. There were, however, a few recalcitrants who were determined to stay in Canada, welcome or unwelcome, reserve or no reserve. Even after Sitting Bull gave up, about 150 lodges remained at Wood Mountain. Some of these Indians later took the long road back to their traditional homeland, and by 1882 only a small band under Black Bull remained encamped near Moose Jaw in Saskatchewan. Finally, in 1913, as a result of the importunities of a Presbyterian clergyman, the Reverend A. D. Pringle, the Department of Indian Affairs in Ottawa granted the remnants of the strong force Sitting Bull had brought to Canada a small reserve near their early location at Wood Mountain. This was the last Sioux reserve established in Canada.[73]

Because the Sioux had no territorial claims in Canada, they did not receive the annuities given the Canadian Indians. They did, however, receive assistance in setting up their reserves similar to that given treaty Indians. The long-term federal government objective was the same in each case—to change the Indians from semi-nomadic, self-supporting buffalo hunters, into sedentary, self-supporting agriculturalists. Self-support was the important thing.[74]

As far as the Sioux were concerned, the odds in favour of the success of Canadian policy were greater than for the Canadian Indians generally. The Sioux had had almost a generation of experience of reserve life in Minnesota; and since coming to British territory in the 1860's they had gained still further agricultural experience by working in the harvest fields of the white settlers in Manitoba.[75] Admittedly the Teton were accustomed to the hunt and to the semi-arid plains of Dakota, but for the bulk of the Sioux in Canada, the country in which they had settled was not greatly dissimilar from that which they had always known in the United States.[76] These two facts may well explain why the early reports of the Canadian Indian agents were invariably enthusiastic about the progress the Sioux Indians were making towards becoming independent farmers. In 1883, for instance, L. W. Herchmer reported that the Oak Lake band were raising corn, potatoes, and turnips and showing themselves to be "excellent workers."[78] The inspector of agencies, in 1890, after a visit to the Bird Tail Creek reserve, wrote, "I have not on any reserve seen so many Indians so diligently employed (each one on his own farm) at one time—the most remarkable point being, that as they have no farmer to oversee them, they set themselves to work and pursue it with such judgement and industry."[78] Edgar Dewdney reported to the superintendent-general of Indian Affairs in 1880 that White Cap had made a good start, and that his men were doing "all they can to assist themselves."[79] One year later, the report was to the effect that the Sioux near Prince Albert had "almost entirely earned their own living" during the winter months by getting out cord wood and had been "no trouble" to the settlers.[80] Reports of a similar tenor were still forthcoming in the nineties. W. R. Tucker, the overseer on White Cap's reserve, informed Ottawa that the Indians were virtually self-supporting, having received no government aid except a few rations of flour and bacon while busy haying.[81] In 1896 J. A. Markle wrote that the Bird Tail Creek Sioux were so "law-abiding, industrious, moral and temperate" that he found it difficult "to believe that they or their forefathers were party to the Minnesota massacre."[82]

It is apparent that, in the first thirty years of the reserve period, the Sioux in Canada made serious efforts to become agriculturalists. Their efforts were not always rewarded. These were the days before the development of early-maturing varieties of grain, and crop failures as a result of early frosts, drought, and grasshoppers were not infrequent. It cannot be surprising that the novice farmers often became discouraged. The whites, too, suffered from the same malaise. That is why a few Saskatchewan Sioux listened to Louis Riel's agitation in 1884 and joined Gabriel Dumont at Fish Creek.[83] Broadly speaking, however, the Sioux in Canada held aloof from the events of 1885, preferring to supplement their uncertain farming efforts by hunting and trapping while the wild game lasted,[84] cutting timber, doing odd jobs and chores for the local settlers, and depending on government rations. We must, therefore, regard the optimistic reports of the Indian agents as valid only to the point that the Sioux were not starving and were able to feed themselves on a day-to-day basis,[85] but not that they were successfully building a firm economic foundation for native society. The worst period was between 1884 and 1895, when there was a succession of dry years. When the rains returned the crops picked up; so too did the spirits of the agents and the Indians. Nevertheless it is probably true that the farm programme would have fallen to pieces during the bad years, had it not been for continued government support.

The school reader and the Bible, along with the plough, were the main pillars of the federal government's acculturation programme. From the outset of the reserve period, Christian denominations were encouraged to open mission schools on Indian reserves. The Presbyterians were already located at Bird Tail Creek when L. W. Herchmer arrived there as Indian agent in 1878. The Anglicans were located at Oak River. Subsequently the Oblate fathers built a day school on the Standing Buffalo reserve; and in 1890 a day school was opened on White Cap's reserve by the Methodists. To avoid denominational rivalry and unnecessary duplication of effort, Ottawa stipulated that the denomination to be in charge of education on any particular reserve was to be that to which the majority of the band members belonged.

The first schools were day schools. When it was found difficult, owing to the scattered nature of Indian settlements, to ensure the regular attendance of Indian children, residential schools replaced them.[86] For over sixty years, from the 1890's to the mid 1960's, the residential school, with its emphasis on manual as well as intellectual skills, and its authoritarian approach, dominated the Indian educational scene in Canada. Since the 1960's the day school has once more returned to favour, this time as a government school with the added currently popular feature of racial integration.

Canadians generally have a naive faith in the virtues of education. They believe that the school can and should act as a corrective to the unfortunate influences of the home. In the case of the Indians, this meant that it was the task of the schoolteacher in the Indian school, day, residential or integrated, to eradicate what he regarded as the less desirable features of the Indian lifestyle and replace them with the more desirable features of the white man's culture: laziness was to give way to industry, uselessness to usefulness, irresponsibility to responsibility. Or in the language of the educationalist, the task of the Indian school was to prepare the Indian "for complete living in their future environment."[87] Because the government looked forward to the ultimate abolition of the reserve, the concession of full political rights, and the "mingling of our Indian people in fullness of personality and privilege among other Canadian citizens,"[88] it saw the duty of the school as one of erasing the "reserve culture" from the minds of the pupils and effecting their transformation into a darker-skinned image of the white man in thought, word, and deed.

·Despite the efforts of the Canadian government—honest and well-meaning in the light of the idealism of an earlier day—to provide the Sioux, as well as other Indian nations living in Western Canada, with a clear-cut philosophy to guide them in their new role in Canadian society, these efforts proved something less than successful. The end product did not turn out as expected. People wondered why not, after the apparent earlier success. Why, after all these years, when they thought they were making the Indian over in their own image, did they find that he was still an Indian?

One explanation may be found in the substantial and unexpected increase in the Indian population, including that of the Sioux, during the present century. In the nineteenth century, the Indian seemed to be a vanishing human species. Certainly, early statistics gave good reason to believe that the Indian would follow the buffalo into oblivion. The high infant mortality rate and the high death rate for adults, largely from pulmonary diseases, provided strong evidence for these dismal convictions. Until the end of the nineteenth century the death rate on the Sioux reserves generally exceeded the birth rate.[89] Indian agents offered as explanations the drastic change from meat to bannock as the principal food of the Indians, and from an outdoor tipi to an indoor log cabin, with resultant scrofula, tuberculosis, and over-indulgence in alcohol.[90] According to the printed reports of the Department of Indian Affairs, the Sioux population of Bird Tail Creek dropped from 143 in 1884 to 74 in 1897, that of Oak Lake from 78 to 32. That of Standing Buffalo dropped from 161 to 153 in the two years between 1895 and 1897.[91] The year 1899 seems to have been the low point of the Sioux population in Canada when it totalled only 897.[92]

This steady decline in numbers reinforced the belief of most whites that the Indians had no future. Even as late as the 1930's, Diamond Jenness felt obliged to write

Doubtless all the tribes will disappear. Some will endure only a few years longer, others, like the Eskimo, may last several centuries. Some will merge steadily with the white race, others will bequeath to future generations only an infinitesimal fraction of their blood.[93]

Even the Indian himself believed this to be his ultimate fate.[94]

V

Then, with the turn of the century, the population curve began to move upwards, probably as a result of improved medical services. At first slowly and then more rapidly the Indian began to recruit his strength; and in the first sixty years of the present century the Sioux population doubled in Canada, reaching a total of 2,193 in 1966-67.[95] The effect has been to give the Indians a new sense of life and a new hope. They were not going to die after all.

But the increase in Indian population brought with it new and serious problems of an economic and social nature. The Sioux reserves in Canada, their size based originally upon the grant of eighty acres for each family of five of a race not expected to survive, are now too small. There is no way the reserves can fulfil the original intention of sustaining a self-supporting agricultural Sioux population. And the problem is compounded by leasing portions of reserve lands to white farmers. Under today's conditions, a viable farm unit on the Canadian Prairies probably requires 640 acres of land, with the trend being towards corporate mega-farms. This means that few Sioux Indians, even those disposed to try, can make a living on the reserves given them by the Canadian government a hundred years ago. The white man's plan to make the Sioux and other Indians self-supporting by farming has now become only a dream. Perhaps that is all it ever was.

Today nearly 30 per cent of the Indians of Manitoba and Saskatchewan live away from their reserves.[96] For the Sioux, the relevant percentages are not much different. In 1976, 75 per cent of the Sioux were reserve Indians; the remaining 25 per cent are living off their reserves. The largest number of Sioux living off the reserve are those belonging to the Standing Buffalo band.[97] These Indians did just what many rural whites have done. Hoping to find employment in industry, they have moved from the country into the towns and cities.

Those off-reserve Indians with a reasonable education have found it possible to make their way into the white-collar group of white society. They have become what E. J. Dosman calls the "affluent" native people. Those who retain their Indian identity have generally taken over the leadership of Indian political movements. Others have tended to identify themselves with the white group of which they have become psychologically a part. The largest group of urban Indians is, however, made up of men and women who lack the educational equipment for anything better than the cheapest unskilled labour.

Since the Second World War, many of Canada's Indians have had to live with problems of poverty, unemployment, boredom, frustration, and destitution. Hence the frequent convictions in the courts for drunkenness, theft, vagrancy, and prostitution, deviations from the laws and norms of the majority group. Insecurity, psychological paralysis, and apathy have become the outward symptoms of the socio-economic life of the "welfare" Indians, a group unable to cope with its environment.[98]

Along with the increase in the Indian population, the present century has witnessed another unexpected development, namely, the growth of Pan-Indianism. With physical survival has come spiritual revival. Perhaps it started when Woodrow Wilson put forward the idea of self-determination as the alternative to colonialism or imperialism. The Iroquois picked up the idea in the early 1920's when Chief Deskaheh of the Grand River reserve at Brantford sought to obtain from the League of Nations formal recognition of the Six Nations as a distinct national entity not subject to Canada. The Iroquois appeal to Geneva failed; but the idea of the Indians as a vital part of North American life made giant strides in Mexico and Central America. In 1940 the first international Pan-Indian congress was held in Patzcuaro. The outcome was the formation of the *Instituto Indigenista Interamerica* and the launching of a quarterly journal and bulletin. Canadians, white and red, ignored the Pan-Indian movement until after the Second World War. Since that time it has spread throughout North America,[99] aided, no doubt, by the inspiration of the independence movements in Africa and the civil rights movement in the United States.

Pan-Indianism today is a positive factor in Indian politics in both Canada and the United States. In Canada it has expressed itself in the various Indian brotherhoods and regional native associations which transcend the traditional tribal boundaries. The first of these was the Allied Tribes of British Columbia, organized in 1915, followed by the League of Indians of Western Canada, formed in Manitoba in 1920. The Native Brotherhood of British Columbia was organized in 1931 and the Indian Association of Alberta in 1939. In 1944 the Saskatchewan Indian Association came into being, and in 1969, the National Indian Brotherhood. Perhaps because they were basically crisis-oriented bodies, the brotherhoods had little or nothing to do with the Mexican or South American organization; but the concept of Pan-Indianism is behind all of these associations, as evinced by the native press in this country.

For some time the Sioux in Canada were impervious to outside influences, including Pan-Indianism. They were inclined to keep to themselves. They did not respond to the Messiah craze or to the peyote cult,[100] both of which enjoyed some popularity in the United States in the late years of the nineteenth century; and they held tightly to their own language to the point where Laviolette was able to write in the 1930's that the Santee dialects were being spoken "even by the children" on the reserves in Manitoba and Saskatchewan. Teton was still in use at Wood Mountain.[101] English was the second language, rather than other Indian tongues, such as the more widely spoken Cree. A number of Sioux customs with respect to family relationships were also being observed at that time as well as certain ritual dances. Thirty-five years later Alice Kehoe was able to cite the instance of a Sioux from the Standing Buffalo reserve, at a meeting of the Federation of Saskatchewan Indians, insisting upon a translation of an address in Cree being made into Sioux.[102] As far as I can discover, few if any Canadian Sioux were involved in the Wounded Knee affair at North Dakota in 1975; and those who have become involved with the American Indian Movement have, almost invariably, been those living off their reserves in the crowded urban areas.[103]

The effect of this linguistic nationalism was to emphasize the Sioux as Sioux rather than as Indians; to discourage close relationships between the

Sioux and other Canadian Indians, and in particular with the dominant Cree. Pan-Indianism, however, has the opposite objective. It is designed to break down tribal isolationism by stressing the common interests of all Indian groups. This means that the Sioux, like the Cree or the Blackfoot, are simply a sub-ethnic group within the larger racial distinction of Indian. Sometimes the loss of this sub-ethnic individualism creates a certain amount of cultural confusion in the minds of Indians and whites alike, as, for instance, when we see a Teton carving a Haida totem pole or a Micmac wearing a Blackfoot feather head-dress. But aside from these cultural sports, Pan-Indianism has given birth to a new sense of direction to the Indian caught up in the vicious circle of frustration, inebriation, and social rebellion. If Pan-Indianism can give the Indian a new self-image, free him from his emotional bondage, then it will have served him well. Perhaps, from Pan-Indianism may grow a new form of native culture, a culture which is a compound of elements derived from traditional sources and from the culture of the Euro-Canadians, a new configuration possessing its own tone and quality—something which will provide a unifying element in native society, and support a future which does not now appear to exist.[104]

But a new self-image is only a starting point. Something more is needed. Social and economic problems cry out for solutions. And these problems have no easy solution. As a historian, and not as a sociologist, a professional administrator, or a political doctrinaire, I offer only a few general, inadequate suggestions.

Certainly, to do away with the reserves is not the answer, for the Indians regard their reserves as their particular pieces of the earth's surface, their basic source of security, their strongest links with the past, a continued reminder to the government that the treaties by which they were established are still in effect. By preference or necessity, many Indians, particularly the older ones, choose to remain on their reserves.[105] Violence may be attractive to the militants; but economic co-operation is evident on many reserves. Greater encouragement could be given to Indian co-operative enterprises, and there could be a much greater degree of Indian input and participation in such matters as schools, social work, police, and health services. Co-operation should go a long way towards eliminating bureaucratic red tape and helping the Indians to help themselves towards what Ellen Fairclough, as minister of northern affairs in 1960, called "social integration."[106]

What of the future?[107] The transition from one lifestyle to another is a long, slow, and often painful process. One wonders if the Indians who have tried to keep the old ways intact—and my innate romanticism places me sympathetically with this group—have merely slowed up a process they cannot stop. This does not imply that responsibility for the generations of maladjustment since the introduction of the treaties rests entirely with those Indians who chose to drag their feet. The white men, too, must bear a share of the blame for their insensitivity to and lack of comprehension of the Indian point of view. The whites would go too far, too fast, and always in the same direction. Recognizing our mutual mistakes, can we achieve mutual understanding? A fraternal, rather than a paternal policy? If that is the way to close the gap of cultures—and such appears to be the philosophy of the Indian Affairs Branch—then the responsibility for its success will rest in the future less upon the federal government than upon the individual white man and Indian in Canada.

> *the great spirit provided for both white and red men*
> *but white man has grown powerful*
> *and defies the gods—*
> *is trying to undo all wakantanka has done.*[108]

Notes

[1]The Caughnawaga were not refugees in the same sense as the others. They were Christian converts among the Mohawks who were persuaded by the Jesuits to leave their traditional home south of the St. Lawrence to go to Canada for the sake of their souls and their skins. See E. J. Devine, *Historic Caughnawaga* (Montreal: Messenger Press, 1922).

[2]See G. F. G. Stanley, "The First Indian Reserves in Canada," *Revue d'Histoire de l'Amérique Française* 4 (1950): 178-210. Also *Indian Treaties and Surrenders from 1680 to 1890* (1892. reprint ed., Ottawa, 1912, facsimile edition, Toronto, 1971).

[3]E. Nurge, *The Modern Sioux, Social Systems and Reservation Culture* (Lincoln: University of Nebraska Press, 1970), p. xii. Anthropologists usually refer to these Indians as "Dakotah," a word meaning "allies," preferring that name to "Sioux," an abbreviation of "Nadouessis" or "Nadouessioux," a French version of "Nadowessiw," an Ojibwa (Chippewa) word meaning "snakes" or, metaphorically, "enemies." Regardless of the pejorative etymology of the word, "Sioux" is too well established to be wished away by pedantic social scientists or by historians with good intentions. In all probability, it will continue to be used by Indians and historians alike, on both sides of the 49th parallel.

[4]The Jesuits wrote, "The Nadouessis, situated to the Northwest or west of the Sault, eighteen days journey farther away.... These people till the soil in the manner of our Hurons, and harvest Indian corn and tobacco." See R. G. Thwaites, ed., *The Jesuit Relations and Allied Documents*, vol. 23 (Cleveland, 1896–1901), pp. 223-27.

[5]The Assiniboine broke away from the Yankton Sioux and aligned themselves with the Cree. Although some authorities suggest that the split came during the seventeenth century, archeological evidence implies an earlier date. See W. M. Hlady, "Indian Migrations in Manitoba and the West," *Manitoba Scientific and Historical Society Papers*, series 3, nos. 17 and 18 (1964): 25, 32.

[6]D. Robinson, *A History of the Dakota or Sioux Indians* (1904. reprint ed., Minneapolis: Ross and Haines, 1956), p. 31.

[7]G. Laviolette, *The Sioux Indians in Canada* (Regina, 1944), p. 25.

[8]See F. G. Roe, *The Indian and the Horse* (Norman: University of Oklahoma Press, 1951) for an account of the impact of the horse upon the economic and social life of the North American Indians.

[9]At a council of Indians at Montreal, 17 August 1778, a number of Sioux chiefs received medals from Governor Frederick Haldimand, including Wabasha, Wankanto, Inyangmanu, Watinyanduta, Waanatan, Wamanza, and Tawahukezononpa. These chiefs represented the seven council fires of the Sioux nation. See Laviolette, *Sioux Indians*, p. 22; and G. F. G. Stanley, "The Indians in the War of 1812," *Canadian Historical Review* 2 (1950): 145–65.

[10]Dickson married the sister of the Yanktonais chief, Red Thunder. Laviolette, *Sioux Indians*, p. 24.

[11]W. Wood, *Select British Documents of the Canadian War of 1812* (Toronto: Champlain Society, 1924), I: 425. Wabasha said, "We live by our English Traders who have always assisted us and never more so than this last year, at the risk of their lives, and we are at all times ready to listen to them on account of the friendship they have always shown us."

[12]Ibid., pp. 436–37: Askin to Claus, 18 July 1812.

[13]A. R. Gilpin, *The War of 1812 in the Old Northwest* (Toronto and East Lansing: Michigan State University Press, 1968), p. 53. The Americans sighted two hundred Sioux warriors at Brownstown.

[14]Some Sisseton and Yanktonais under Waanatan were at Fort Meigs. Waanatan was made a captain and was taken to England and presented to the king. See Laviolette, *Sioux Indians*, p. 24.

[15]Wood, *Select British Documents*, III: 250, 251, 254, 261: Wabasha to Roberts, 5 February 1813; Lambton to Roberts, 10 February 1813; McDouall to Drummond, 16 July 1814; McKay to McDouall, 27 July 1814.

[16]D. McNickle, *The Indian Tribes of the United States, Ethnic and Cultural Survival* (London: Oxford University Press, 1962), pp. 35, 38. Also, E. B. Leacock and N. O. Lurie, *North American Indians in Historical Perspective* (New York: Random House, 1971), p. 212.

[17]Not all Americans shared the popular point of view. Senator Theodore Frelinghuysen of New Jersey addressed the Senate for two days on the moral aspects of the American policy, and Congressman Storrs argued against the hypocrisy of pretending that the move was for the benefit of the Indians. See D. Van Every, *Disinherited: The Lost Birthright of the American Indian* (New York: Morrow, 1966), ch. 9.

[18]McNickle, *Indian Tribes*, pp. 43–44. In all fairness it should be pointed out that the courts in the United States did continue to respect the validity of the treaties which had previously been incorporated into the law of the land. There are numerous instances in which the courts awarded monetary judgments to Indian tribes for actions taken by the United States government or its agents in violation of treaty stipulations. See also, F. S. Cohen, "Tribal Property," in *Handbook of Federal Indian Law* (Washington, 1941), ch. 15.

[19]There were two treaties, one concluded at Traverse des Sioux with the Sisseton and Wahpeton and the other at Mendota, with Wahpekute and Mdewakantonwan.

[20]F. W. Seymour, *The Story of the Red Man* (London: Tudor, 1929), p. 273. See also W. W. Folwell, *A History of Minnesota* (St. Paul: Minnesota Historical Society, 1956), vol. 1, p. 202.

[21]T. C. Blegen, *Minnesota, a History of the State* (Minneapolis: University of Minnesota Press, 1963), p. 261. See also D. Brown, *Bury My Heart at Wounded Knee, an Indian History of the American West* (New York: Holt, Rinehart, Winston, 1970), pp. 42–43.

[22]Blegen, *Minnesota*, p. 170.

[23]Governor Alexander Ramsey declared in his message to the legislature on 9 September 1862, "The Sioux Indians of Minnesota must be exterminated or driven forever beyond the borders of the state." See Blegen, *Minnesota*, p. 280. Bishop Whipple bought some land along the Mississippi and invited Episcopalian Santee to take possession of it. They clustered at Prairie Island about seventeen miles north of Red Wing in Minnesota. Eventually they lost their lands, when the property reverted to the government for non-payment of taxes. R. Landes, *The Mystic Lake Sioux, Sociology of the Mdewakantonwan Santee* (Madison: University of Wisconsin Press, 1968), ch. 1. See also R. W. Meyer, "The Prairie Island Community: A Remnant of Minnesota Sioux," *Minnesota History* 37 (1961): 271–82.

[24]Little Crow was killed while on a hunting trip in Minnesota. Twenty-five dollars bounty was being offered by Minnesota for Sioux scalps. The two men who killed Little Crow received the regular bounty, plus a bonus of five hundred dollars. See Brown, *Wounded Knee*, pp. 62–63; also W. N. Trenerry, "The Shooting of Little Crow, Heroism or Murder?" *Minnesota*

History 38 (1962): 152–53; and P. I. Wellman, *The Indian Wars of the West* (Garden City, N.Y.: Doubleday, 1963), pp. 36–37.

[25]Seymour, *Story of the Red Man*, p. 301.

[26]Brown, *Wounded Knee*, p. 261.

[27]*New York Herald*, 27 August, 25 September 1874.

[28]E. E. Rich, *The History of the Hudson's Bay Company 1670–1870* (London: Hudson's Bay Record Society, 1959), II: 425, 539, 554. Nettley Creek, which runs into the Red River, was once called Rivière aux Morts, from a massacre of the Saulteaux by the Sioux. See A. S. Morton, *A History of the Canadian West* (London, [n.d.]), p. 431.

[29]W. L. Morton, "The Battle at the Grand Coteau, 13–14 July 1851," *Manitoba Scientific and Historical Society Papers*, series 3, no. 16 (1961): 37–49. See also, H. de Trémaudan, *Histoire de la Nation Métisse* (Montréal: A. Lévesque, 1935), pp. 143–45.

[30]A. S. Morton, *History of the Canadian West*, p. 829. See also, G. F. G. Stanley, *Canada's Soldiers* (Toronto, 1974), p. 208.

[31]*Nor'Wester*, 15 November 1861.

[32]E. H. Oliver, ed., *The Canadian North West: Its Early Development and Legislative Records*, Canadian Archives Publication No. 9 (Ottawa, 1914), I: 511–13. See also, A. C. Gluek, "The Sioux Uprising, A Problem in International Relations," *Minnesota History* 34 (1955): 317–24.

[33]*Copies or Extracts of All the Correspondence … representing a Tribe of Sioux Indians who were Refugees within the British-Territories*, House of Commons, 1864 (Great Britain), p. 4: Dallas to Fraser, 11 December 1863.

[34]Several Sioux children whose parents had been killed were taken care of by the settlers and by the Grey Nuns at St. François Xavier.

[35]*Extracts of Correspondence*, p. 5: Dallas to Fraser, 18 December 1863.

[36]Ibid., p. 6: Head to Rogers, 4 March 1864. With this letter Head enclosed extracts of newspaper accounts giving details of the kidnapping.

[37]*Canadian News*, 3 March 1864.

[38]Folwell, *Minnesota*, II: 293.

[39]*Extracts of Correspondence*, pp. 13–14: Hatch to Dallas, 4 March 1864; Dallas to Hatch, 7 March 1864. For an example of the pressure brought to bear on Dallas, see the report of a public meeting held in the court room of Red River, 15 February 1864. The meeting was in favour of delivering the Sioux to the Americans at Pembina as "the only means of securing permanent safety from the Sioux." The resolutions were signed by A. G. B. Bannantyne, John Schultz, Thomas Thomas and Alban Fidler. See pp. 9–12: Head to Fortescue, 11 April 1864 with enclosures.

[40]Gluek, "Sioux Uprising," p. 324. Gluek writes of Hatch, "In the end, he proved to be no Andrew Jackson, and, permission notwithstanding, he dared not cross an international line in pursuit of Indians."

[41]*Extracts of Correspondence*, p. 13: Dallas to the Sioux chiefs, 20 February 1864.

[42]*Nor'Wester*, 16 September 1864. Hargrave, writing six years later, was inclined to believe that many of these depredations, including the theft of religious objects from the churches, were committed by local Indians rather than by the Sioux. See J. J. Hargrave, *Red River* (Montreal: the author, 1871), p. 340.

[43]Laviolette, *Sioux Indians*, p. 68.

[44]*Opening up the West, being the Official Reports of the North West Mounted Police 1874–1881* (Facsimile edition, Toronto, 1973), p. 28: Walsh to Macleod, 31 December 1876.

[45]Ibid., p. 32: Walsh to Irvine, 15 March 1877.

[46]C. W. de Keweit and F. H. Underhill, *Dufferin-Carnarvon Correspondence, 1874–1878* (Toronto: Champlain Society, 1955), p. 254: Dufferin to Carnarvon, 29 July 1876.

[47]*Official Reports of the North West Mounted Police*, p. 33: Irvine to Scott, 23 May 1877.

[48]Ibid., p. 35: Macleod to Mackenzie, 30 May 1876.

[49]S. F. Bemis, *The American Secretaries of State and their Diplomacy* (1927–29. reprint ed., New York: Cooper Square, 1958), p. 227.

[50]C. F. Turner, *Across the Medicine Line* (Toronto: McClelland & Stewart, 1973), p. 103. See R.C.M.P. file on Sitting Bull, vol. 4: J. B. Mitchell to J. P. Turner, 19 August 1941.

[51]*Official Reports of the North West Mounted Police*, p. 41, E. D. Clark report on a council held 2 June 1877 at Sitting Bull's camp.

52*Dufferin–Carnarvon Correspondence*, pp. 362, 368: Dufferin to Carnarvon, 25 August 1877; Dufferin to Carnarvon, 9 October 1877.

53*Debates of the House of Commons*, Ottawa, 1878, p. 37. For a discussion of the diplomatic side of the Sitting Bull episode see G. Pennanen, "Sitting Bull, Indian Without a Country," *Canadian Historical Review* 51 (1970), pp. 123–40.

54*Official Reports of the North West Mounted Police*, p. 42: Scott to Macleod, 15 August 1877.

55Cited in P. Sharp, *Whoop-Up Country* (Minneapolis: University of Minnesota Press, 1955), pp. 268–69.

56S. Steele, *Forty Years in Canada* (Toronto, 1914), p. 129.

57*The Globe*, 16 August 1877. Walsh felt that the Americans were trying to embroil Canada in an Indian war. "We should have no understanding with them," he wrote. "They would be pleased if they could embroil us. . . . The cost of an Indian war in such a country as ours would be enormous." See Turner, *Across the Medicine Lines*, pp. 149–50.

58Macdonald believed that Evarts's attitude was mere political posturing in view of a forthcoming election. "I am sure," he wrote, "that Evarts would be delighted to distinguish his tenure of office, by consumating an act which would be extremely popular throughout the United States." See W. S. McNutt, *Days of Lorne* (Fredericton: Brunswick Press, 1955), p. 74.

59N. A. Miles, *Personal Recollections and Observations of General Nelson A. Miles* (Chicago: Werner, 1896), p. 309.

60Turner, *Across the Medicine Line*, p. 180.

61F. Wade, "Jean Louis Légaré's Story," *Canadian Magazine*, February 1905, p. 338. See also, G. MacEwan, *Sitting Bull, the Years in Canada* (Edmonton, 1973) and the "Report of the Commissioner of the North West Mounted Police for 1880."

62C. F. Turner, "Sitting Bull Tests the Mettle of the Redcoats," in H. Dempsey, *Men in Scarlet* (Calgary: Historical Society of Alberta, [n.d.]), p. 76. Even Walsh did not consider that Sitting Bull should have a reserve in Canada. See P.A.C., RG 10, vol. 3691, folder 13893: Walsh to Macdonald, 11 September 1880.

63Ottawa was disturbed by the Indian unrest in the west arising out of the Riel troubles of 1869–70 and the arrangements for the survey of the boundary line between Canada and the United States. See Canada, *Sessional Papers*, no. 23, 1873, p. 14: Morris to the secretary of state for the provinces, 13 December 1872. See also A. Morris, *The Treaties of Canada with the Indians of Manitoba and the North West Territories* (Toronto: Belfords, Clarke, 1880), introduction. For a study of Canada's treaty system, see A. G. Harper, "Canada's Indian Administration: The Treaty System," *América Indígena* 7, (April 1947): 129–48.

64Morris, *Treaties of Canada*, p. 288.

65It should be noted that the Sioux held aloof from the events in Red River 1869–70, despite the activities of George (Shawman) Racette and J. S. Dennis. See W. L. Morton, *Alexander Begg's Red River Journal* (Toronto: Champlain Society, 1956), pp. 73, 198, 350–51.

66Canada, *Sessional Papers*, no. 23, 1873, p. 13: Morris to the secretary of state for the provinces, 13 December 1872. Morris wrote, "I think it would be wise to give them a reserve." Archibald's despatch of 27 December 1871 is mentioned in the Morris letter. Morris made it quite clear that any reserve would be given "not as a matter of right but of grace." See P.A.C., Morris Papers, MG 27 C8, memorandum, 30 December 1873.

67Canada, *Sessional Papers*, no. 9, 1876, p. xi: "Report of the Minister of the Interior," 31 January 1876. See also ibid., p. 42: Provencher to the superintendent-general of Indian Affairs, 30 October 1875.

68In 1934 some twenty-three families were moved from Portage to the Long Plains reserve but few remained there. Most of them returned to Portage or moved to Oak Lake. See Laviolette, *Sioux Indians*, pp. 114–15.

69Canada, *Sessional Papers*, no. 10, 1878, p. xvii: report of the Hon. David Mills, 31 December 1877. The reserve was surveyed in 1878.

70Indian Department officials never regarded this reserve as much of a success. J. A. Markle of the Birtle Agency reported in July 1896 that there were only twenty-nine Indians there. He also complained that it was too close to the United States and was becoming a meeting place for "scalawag" Indians. See Canada, *Sessional Papers*, no. 14, 1897, p. 145. The reserve was surrendered in 1907 and the inhabitants moved to Oak Lake.

[71]Canada, *Sessional Papers*, no. 9, 1876, p. xxvii: "Report of the Minister of the Interior," 31 January 1876.

[72]Ibid., no. 7, 1879, p. 58: Laird to the superintendent-general of Indian Affairs, 5 December 1878.

[73]Laviolette, *Sioux Indians*, p. 123, n. 15. An effort was made during the 1890's to convince the Indians they should go back to the United States, to the extent of proposing they should be removed by force. However, it was recognized that they had remained quietly in Canada since the 1870's, spending the summers in the vicinity of Moose Jaw, where they were a source of cheap farm labour. No strong arm action was taken to send them back to the United States or compel them to join White Cap's band at Moose Woods. See P.A.C., RG 10, 3652: Hayter Reed memorandum on the refugee Sioux at Moose Jaw, 15 March 1897.

[74]Self-support continued to be the government's objective. In 1933 the general instructions sent to Indian agents in Canada (form 1024, 1 September 1933) said, "It may be stated as a first principle that it is the policy of the Department to promote self-support." See A. G. Harper, "Canada's Indian Administration: Basic Concepts and Objectives," *América Indígena* 5, (April 1945): 119-32.

[75]R. W. Meyer, "The Canadian Sioux—Refugees from Minnesota," *Minnesota History* (Spring 1968): 20.

[76]A. Kehoe, "The Dakotas in Saskatchewan," in E. Nurge, *Modern Sioux*, p. 149.

[77]Canada, *Sessional Papers*, no. 4, 1884, p. 65: L. W. Herchmer to the superintendent-general of Indian Affairs, 30 June 1883.

[78]Canada, *Sessional Papers*, no. 18, 1891, p. 158: F. Wadsworth to the superintendent-general of Indian Affairs, 30 October 1890.

[79]Canada, *Sessional Papers*, no. 4, 1880, p. 98: E. Dewdney to the superintendent-general of Indian Affairs, 2 January 1880.

[80]Canada, *Sessional Papers*, no. 6, 1882, p. ix: report of the Carlton Indian Agency, 23 March 1881.

[81]Canada, *Sessional Papers*, no. 14, 1897, pp. 186-87: W. R. Tucker to the superintendent-general of Indian Affairs, 31 June 1896.

[82]Ibid., p. 143: Markle to the superintendent-general of Indian Affairs, 30 July 1896.

[83]Canada, *Sessional Papers*, no. 52, 1886, pp. 33-60: Queen vs. White Cap (Wah-pah-iss-co). See also ibid., pp. 2-13: Queen vs. Oka-doka et al. This group included Red Eagle, a Sioux Indian from the White Cap band.

[84]After the buffalo disappeared from the prairies, neither deer, antelope, nor wild fowl existed in sufficient numbers to support the Indians.

[85]Meyer, "Prairie Island Community," p. 22. For the degree of self-sufficiency attained by the Indians see Canada, *Sessional Papers*, no. 14, 1894, p. 56: Lash to the superintendent-general of Indian Affairs, 9 September 1893; Canada, *Sessional Papers*, no. 14, 1895, p. 58: Lash to the superintendent-general of Indian Affairs, 31 August 1894; Canada, *Sessional Papers*, no. 18, 1891, p. 43: Markle to the superintendent-general of Indian Affairs, 18 August 1890; Canada, *Sessional Papers*, no. 14, 1898, pp. 123-26: Markle to the superintendent-general of Indian Affairs, 30 June 1897.

[86]When the Hudson's Bay Company sent the Rev. John West to Red River in 1820, West obtained a grant from the Church Missionary Society which made it possible for him to establish an Indian school. West may be considered as the father of the Indian residential school system in Western Canada. Hayter Reed, the deputy superintendent-general of Indian Affairs, reported 2 December 1895 on the indifference of the Indians to day schools. See Canada, *Sessional Papers*, no. 14, 1896, p. xxii.

[87]A. E. Wescott, "Curricula for Indian Schools," in C. T. Loram and T. F. McIlwraith, *The North American Indian Today* (Toronto: University of Toronto Press, 1943), p. 283.

[88]J. F. Woodsworth, "Problems of Indian Education in Canada," in Loram and McIlwraith, *The North American Indian Today*, p. 266.

[89]Meyer, "Prairie Island Community," *North American Indian*, p. 23.

[90]Canada, *Sessional Papers*, no. 4, 1884, p. 64: Herchmer to the superintendent-general, 30 June 1883; Canada, *Sessional Papers*, no. 4, 1886, p. 61: Herchmer to the superintendent-general, 4 October 1885; Canada, *Sessional Papers*, no. 18, 1891, p. 43: Markle to the superintendent-general, 18 August 1890.

[91]Canada, *Sessional Papers*, no. 14, 1896, pp. 364–65; Canada, *Sessional Papers*, no. 14, 1898, p. 367.

[92]Meyer, "Prairie Island Community," p. 26.

[93]D. Jenness, *The Indians of Canada*, National Museum of Canada, Bulletin No. 65, 2nd ed. (Ottawa, [n.d.]), p. 264.

[94]J. Collier, "The United States Indian Administration as a Laboratory of Ethnic Relations," *Social Research* 12 (1945): 271–73.

[95]*Report of the Department of Indian Affairs and Northern Development*, Indian Affairs Branch, 1967, pp. 14–16. Here are the figures given for the various reserves, *Manitoba*—Birdtail Creek, 185; Long Plains, 204; Oak Lake, 244; Oak River, 807: *Saskatchewan*—Wahpaton, 84; Moose Woods (White Cap), 132; Standing Buffalo, 473; Wood Mountain 64. Compare figures in Nurge, *Modern Sioux*, p. 304. E. J. Dosman, *Indians: The Urban Dilemma* (Toronto: McClelland & Stewart, 1972), p. 25, gives the Sioux population of Saskatchewan in 1971 as Standing Buffalo, 519; Wahpaton, 86; Moose Woods, 156; Wood Mountain, 71. No figures are available for Manitoba.

[96]*Canada Year Book, 1975* (Ottawa, 1975), p. 170, table 4.22. Those Indians living on reserves in Manitoba number 29,938, off reserves, 10,140; in Saskatchewan, on reserves 27,214, off reserves, 11,655, for a total on reserves of 57,152, off reserves 21,795. The percentage of Alberta Indians on reserves is higher. Only 5,574 Indians live off the reserves and 24,295 on the reserves. Indians leave the reserves basically for economic reasons and partly because of a wish to be self-reliant. See J. S. Frideres, *Canada's Indian Contemporary Conflicts* (Scarborough, Ont.: Prentice-Hall, 1974), pp. 88–92. Some Indians who had served in the armed forces moved to the cities and encouraged other Indians to do so.

[97]The relevant statistics for 1976 are as follows

Band	On Reserve	Off Reserve	Total
Bird Tail	174	52	226
Sioux Valley (Oak River)	820	189	1009
Oak Lake	235	72	307
Dakota Plains	104	28	132
Dakota Tipi	140	85	225
Moose Woods	126	45	171
Wahpaton	85	15	100
Standing Buffalo	362	236	598
Wood Mountain	37	36	73

These figures were provided the author by the Indian Affairs Branch, Ottawa.

[98]Heather Robertson suggests that when the Indians settled on their reserves in the early years the consumption of alcohol declined because they "were assured of protection and sufficient food." See *Reservations Are For Indians* (Toronto: Lewis and Samuel, 1970), p. 278. I would also add, because the Indians were actively employed. Miss Robertson also maintains that the Indian drinking problem increased "in direct proportion to the Indians' dependency on welfare" (ibid.), which is just another way of saying because of the lack of gainful employment for Indians. She is quite right in pointing out that the economy which the Indians built up in the early treaty years is "now obsolete and the Indian is, yet once more faced with starvation and extinction.... It is this friction between the Indian's own desire to adapt, his fear of change, and impositions which the government places on him that produces alcoholism" (p. 279). The tragedy is that the Indians' excessive drinking is self-defeating.

[99]E. Palmer Patterson II, *The Canadian Indian: The History Since 1500* (Don Mills, Ont.: Collier-Macmillan Canada, 1972), p. 5. As far as the Pan-Indian movement is concerned, I drew attention to this phenomenon in a paper to the Canadian Historical Association in 1952. See *Annual Report* (1952): p. 21.

[100]Laviolette, *Sioux Indians*, pp. 126–27. The Ghost Dance ritual is still carried on by the older generation of Sioux in Saskatchewan, although Alice Kehoe says that it "seems destined to die out after this generation." See Kehoe, "Dakotas in Saskatchewan," p. 163. It was the Messiah craze that led to the shooting of Sitting Bull in 1890. See Turner, *Across the Medicine Line*, pp. 256–60.

[101]Laviolette, *Sioux Indians*, p. 125.

[102] Kehoe, "Dakotas in Saskatchewan," p. 171.

[103] This information was provided the author by the Indian Affairs Branch, Ottawa.

[104] There is still some argument as to whether the Canadian Indians constitute an ethnic group or a cultural minority. Hitherto, Canadian Indians have not shared a common cultural tradition. Their lifestyles have varied according to their geographical and economic backgrounds. See M. Nagler, *Natives Without a Home* (Don Mills, Ont.: Longmans, 1975), pp. xv, xvi, 1–2, and Patterson, *Canadian Indian*, p. 59.

[105] H. Cardinal, *The Unjust Society* (Edmonton: Hurtig, 1970), p. 28. Cardinal writes, "These treaties represent an Indian magna carta."

[106] Dosman, *Indians*, p. 27. Of the five hundred native schools under federal jurisdiction, local band councils control only nineteen or twenty. The National Indian Brotherhood is seeking for the Indian bands the same kind of control a local school board would have. One of the objections to using native teachers has been met in Manitoba by a special five-year programme to train native teachers. This programme involves Indians working in reserve schools as teaching assistants during the academic year and taking teacher training courses for ten weeks in the summer. See V. Kirkness, Education Director, National Indian Brotherhood, in *Micmac News*, 8 October 1976, p. 5.

[107] Some people consider assimilation ultimately inevitable. See A. K. Davis "Urban Indians Within Canada," *Transactions of the Royal Society of Canada*, Series 4 (1968), vol. 6, p. 228; and R. Underhill, *Red Man's America, a History of Indians in the United States* (Chicago: University of Chicago Press, 1963), p. 341. The Indians living on reserves may resist assimilation and retain something of their own value system; the urban Indians, by moving away from the reserves, reject ancestral patterns. They risk becoming assimilated. Assimilation is still optional with Canadian Indians. See Nagler, *Natives Without a Home*, p. 17. When I first did research in the Department of Indian Affairs in those far off days of the 1930's, when Dr. McGill of Calgary was deputy minister of Indian Affairs in Ottawa, I wondered why there were no Indians in the Indian Department. I still wonder why the Indian Branch never became a career service for Indians.

[108] "Poem to Sitting Bull and his son Crowfoot," in Andrew Suknaski, *Wood Mountain Poems* (Toronto: Macmillan, 1976), p. 67.

7

Prairie Canadians' Orientations towards Indians*

ROGER GIBBINS AND J. RICK PONTING

The treaties signed between the Plains Indians and the federal government are an example of what sociologists call "accommodative structures."[1] An "accommodative structure" is a *modus vivendi*—an agreement to cease conflict or competition so that other goals may be pursued by each party or so that the losses of each party may be minimized. As accommodative structures, the treaties with the Canadian Plains tribes during the 1870's provided the Indians with the essentials of physical sustenance with certain legal rights and protections, in exchange for their lands and their promise to keep the peace. In addition there were socio-economic, territorial, administrative, and political aspects to the accommodation reached between the Indians and the government. For their part, Indians were relegated to reserves and placed under the control of a bureaucratic apparatus created in 1879 and headed by Indian Commissioner Edgar Dewdney. By the terms of the 1876 Indian Act, Indians were denied the franchise in federal or provincial elections and thus were excluded from the political process.

With the signing of the treaties, Indians were excluded not only from politics but from most other areas of Canadian life. The reserves, coupled with the geographical isolation of most Indian communities, threw up a barrier between the Indian and non-Indian societies that was rarely breached. However, some seventy-five years after the treaties were signed conditions began to change in significant ways. In particular, tremendous technological advances in the mass media ended the isolation of the Indian society. Indian people became exposed to the ideologies of decolonization in Third World countries, and, closer to home, to the instructive examples of other minorities (notably the blacks and Indians in the United States) who vigorously challenged their oppressors in order to arrive at a new accommodation. They

* The research upon which this article is based was funded by grants from the Donner Canadian Foundation and The University of Calgary. This article is reprinted with permission, and in revised form, from *Prairie Forum* 2, no. 1 (1977): 57–81.

further witnessed the revival of these other groups' cultures and the emergence of social movements to promote their demands. The example of these other peoples helped rekindle a sense of hope in Canadian Indians, and with this, the accommodative structures began to weaken. The granting of the federal franchise in 1960 cracked the political pillar of the accommodative structures, while the baby "boom" of the 1960's and the resultant population pressure on the reserves cracked the territorial pillar, as increasing numbers of Indians left the reserves and came to the cities.[2] In addition, a determination arose to challenge the government on its violation of the legal provisions of the treaties and to take full advantage of the legal system which had been imposed upon them in order to retrieve lost lands and to secure a more viable economic base for themselves.

An amorphous social movement, led by a plethora of national and provincial native organizations, arose across the country. One of its main objects of attack was the last pillar of the old accommodative structure—the bureaucracy represented by the Department of Indian Affairs and Northern Development. While the tactics followed by the different branches of this social movement varied considerably, they all—along with the movement's rhetoric, demands, and accomplishments—helped propel Indians out of the state of virtual "irrelevance"[3] into which the accommodative structures of the treaties had placed them *vis-à-vis* the non-Indian society.

Lead by a new generation of leaders, Indians have moved from the wings much closer to the centre of the political stage in Canada. The questions thus arise as to how Canadian Indians are now perceived by non-Indians, how favourably (or unfavourably) disposed Canadians are toward Indians, and how the strategies, tactics, and goals pursued by Indians or available to them are received by non-Indians.

If new accommodative structures are to be forged between Indians and governments, the shape and character of those structures may be influenced by the perceptions and orientations toward Indians held by non-Indians in the electorate. For instance, if a "white backlash" were to occur against the Indian movement, the tactical options available to the movement would likely be considerably reduced, with concomitant effects upon the movement's ability to achieve its goals. As a minority, Indians are vulnerably exposed to the consequences of adverse public opinion.

In Western Canada, where the proportion of Indians in the population is greater than in the eastern provinces, there is considerable potential for the emergence of new accommodative structures, as illustrated by the 1976 agreement between the Alberta government, provincial native organizations, and the Syncrude corporation to permit Indian participation in the development of the Athabasca tar sands. In light of this potential, it is our purpose here first to describe the general perceptions which westerners hold of native Indians. Then we shall examine non-Indian reactions to native land claims—

claims which often constitute the foundation of the new accommodative structures which natives are trying to erect. Thirdly, we shall discuss white reactions to the use of several different tactics which Indians have at their disposal in trying to achieve their goals. In concluding, we shall explore some factors which have the potential ability to change westerners' sentiments toward Indians in the future.

The data to be used in this endeavour come from a national study conducted during January and February 1976. At that time, 1,832 randomly selected residents of Canada living coast to coast and south of the sixtieth parallel of latitude were interviewed in their homes for approximately one hour, primarily on the topic of their orientations toward Indians and Indian issues in Canada. Our attention in this paper will be focused mainly upon the 676 respondents interviewed in the Prairie provinces. Although passing reference will be made to results from the rest of Canada, so as to provide a comparative context for the Western data, space constraints preclude our dwelling upon these comparisons.

GENERAL PERCEPTIONS OF CANADIAN INDIANS

Differences Between Native Indians and Other Canadians

The first question in the interview which dealt directly with Indians was as follows: "If we were to compare native Canadian Indians with other Canadians, in your opinion, what would be the major differences between them?" For the Western Canadian sample, 80 per cent of the respondents cited at least one difference which they perceived to exist between Indians and other Canadians.

Open-ended questions of this type are very useful since responses are not pre-structured and the respondent is forced to rely upon his or her own thoughts and images. It must be stressed, however, that the task of reducing over five hundred responses, ranging from the cryptic to the convoluted, to manageable categories or codes is not an easy one. We feel, nevertheless, that the eleven codes listed in Table 1 do not inflict excessive violence upon the complexity and nuances of individual perceptions.

Table 1 shows the frequency with which various differences between Indians and non-Indians were mentioned. As the reader will note, respondents from the three Prairie provinces have not been segregated; such separation will be used only when interprovincial differences are statistically significant. Thus when interprovincial differences are not cited the reader can assume that the attitudes of the Prairie population are not differentiated along provincial lines.

TABLE 1

MAJOR DIFFERENCES BETWEEN NATIVE CANADIAN INDIANS
AND OTHER CANADIANS*

*Per Cent Mentioning***

Difference Mentioned	Prairie Sample	National Non-Prairie
1) Differences emphasizing Indian personality deficiencies (e.g.: laziness, lack of ambition, lack of initiative)	33.1	17.3
2) Differences in education	24.1	24.7
3) Differences in culture, heritage, or lifestyle (e.g.: "upbringing," "way of life," "philosophy of life")	18.7	27.5
4) Discrimination and/or prejudice mentioned as a difference	15.9	16.7
5) Differences in economic opportunities or lack of economic achievement (e.g.: unemployment, inappropriate skills or training)	14.7	17.3
6) Differences in government treatment	13.8	10.8
7) Poverty or poor living conditions of Indians (e.g.: low incomes, poor health or nutrition, poor housing, poor sanitation)	13.0	17.3
8) Differences in the use of alcohol	7.7	3.1
9) Differences related to problems of assimilation and adjustment (e.g.: inability or unwillingness to assimilate and adjust, loss of identity)	7.0	4.6
10) Indian remoteness, geographical or social, from the Canadian society	5.6	12.2
11) Indian relationship to the natural environment (e.g.: Indians protect, appreciate or know more about the environment, Indians live closer to the land)	1.5	4.0

* "If we were to compare native Canadian Indians with other Canadians, in your opinion what would be the major differences between them?"

** Because multiple answers were possible, the percentages do not total to 100 per cent. The percentages in this table are based upon the 554 Prairie respondents and 819 national non-Prairie respondents who stated at least one difference between Indians and other Canadians.

Table 1 shows that among the Prairie residents the most frequently mentioned differences referred to what, from the respondent's point of view, might be called "personality deficiencies" among native Indians. Although most of the references related in one manner or another to laziness, lack of initiative, or lack of motivation, sundry other "faults" were also mentioned. The frequency with which personality differences were mentioned suggests a current of pejorative ethnic stereotyping among the Western Canadian population. However, the next six most frequently mentioned differences cited by Prairie respondents in Table 1 seem less pejorative in their content. For example, the fact that Indians are perceived as less educated or as lacking sufficient economic opportunities does not necessarily imply racial hostility.

Such perceptions could spring from an acute awareness of, and sympathy for, the native peoples as readily as they could from prejudice. Closely related to the question on the main differences between Indians and other Canadians was the following:

> Some people say that Indians have to choose between either having a higher standard of living or preserving their traditional way of life. Do you agree that they have to make a choice or can they have both?

Here, a bare majority (53.7 per cent) of our Prairie respondents indicated that they felt that Indians could have both while a large minority (42.2 per cent) felt that a choice would have to be made. Among those respondents who felt that a choice was necessary, a slight majority (55.8 per cent) indicated that, in their view, the majority of Indians would choose to preserve their way of life. Conversely, 37.9 per cent were of the opinion that the majority of Indians would choose a higher standard of living.

Main Problems Faced by Canadian Indians

The perceptions captured in Table 1 are to some extent modified, and to some extent reinforced, by answers to the next question in the interview which asked: "What would you say are the *main problems* faced by Canadian Indians today?" Ninety-five per cent of the respondents mentioned at least one problem, with the majority mentioning more than one.

While this question posed coding difficulties similar to those encountered for the "main differences" question, the vast majority of responses have been incorporated in the codes presented in Table 2. There we observe that prejudice and discrimination by others constituted the most frequently mentioned problem facing Canadian Indians today, followed closely by problems related to alcohol and less closely by problems centering about educational "deficiencies."[4] The set of problems ranked fourth in frequency dealt with political or governmental problems. Interestingly, the great majority (78 per cent) of responses thus coded focused upon government assistance to Indians, assistance which was frequently said to rob Indians of ambition and self-reliance. Only a single respondent touched upon Indians' lack of political power. It seems, then, that the very acute political problems that Indians face in their dealings with all levels of government have not penetrated the perceptual filters of Western Canadians.

Taken alone, neither this nor the question involving the main differences between Indians and other Canadians is a satisfactory tool for fully identifying the stereotypes of Indians held by Western Canadians. However, the results obtained are quite similar to those reported by Mackie[5] from a study of stereotypes about Indians which she conducted in Edmonton during the period 1968–1970. Respondents in her study also focused upon what we have called "personality deficiencies," as well as upon Indians' low level of education, their rejection or oppression by non-Indians, their poverty, and their problems with alcohol. However, lest this discussion leave the impression that there is a consensus in Western Canada on the attributes of Indians, it should be noted that in the open-ended questions of both our study and Mackie's no single attribute or problem was cited by more than a third of the sample. Caution is also in order in making inferences about non-Indians' evaluations of Indians on the basis of data such as ours or Mackie's. For instance, the mention of characteristics such as alcoholism

TABLE 2

MAIN PROBLEMS FACED BY CANADIAN INDIANS TODAY*

*Per Cent Mentioning***

Problem Mentioned	Prairie Sample	National Non-Prairie
1) Prejudice and/or discrimination against Canadian Indians (Also: racism, bigotry, lack of acceptance by whites)	31.0	40.6
2) Drinking and/or alcoholism	28.6	8.7
3) Lack of education (Also: dropping out of school, lack of an appropriate education)	23.9	24.2
4) Political and/or governmental problems (e.g.: government assistance, too much welfare, dependency, government interference in Indian lives)	22.0	16.2
5) Poverty, unemployment, and lack of economic opportunities	19.0	27.3
6) Personality "deficiencies" (e.g.: laziness, lack of initiative, shyness, low self-esteem, feelings of inferiority)	19.0	12.7
7) Problems of assimilation and adjustment (Including: inability or unwillingness to assimilate, forced assimilation, loss of culture, identity problems)	17.5	19.1
8) Indian reserves (e.g.: reserves hold Indians back, prevent integration, cannot be economically self-sufficient)	7.4	10.7
9) Problems of internal organization and cohesion (e.g.: lack of leadership, cannot agree among themselves, internal bickering)	2.8	1.7

* "What would you say are the main problems faced by Canadian Indians today?... Are there any other problems you can think of?"

** As multiple answers were possible, the percentages do not total to 100 per cent. The percentages in this table are based upon the 642 Prairie respondents and 1,016 national non-Prairie respondents who stated at least one problem.

is hard to assess without knowing whom the respondent holds responsible for these characteristics—the Indians themselves or the larger society. The responses in Tables 1 and 2 would lead us to hypothesize that, with regard to stereotypes held by the Western Canadian adult population, neither a positive nor a negative evaluation of native Indians predominates. Looking to the future, if Indians achieve a new economic accommodation with white society and improve their level of economic development and their physical standard of living, the perceptions and evaluations which some non-Indians hold of them may change in a "positive" direction.

CONTACT WITH CANADIAN INDIANS

The sociological literature clearly indicates that intergroup attitudes are affected by the characteristics of interpersonal contact between group members.[6] In order to assess the impact of interpersonal contact upon perceptions of Canadian Indians, we asked our respondents if, either now or in the past, they had come into contact with Indians in any of five situations. On the whole, the extent of contact thus indicated was quite extensive. Fifty-seven per cent reported contact with Indians living in their neighbourhood, 55 per cent reported contact at work, 40 per cent cited a close friend who was an Indian, 24 per cent reported contact in clubs or organizations, and 11 per cent of the Prairie sample mentioned Indian relatives. On the average, Prairie respondents reported at least two of the five types of contact, compared to an average of only one for non-Prairie respondents.

Interestingly, we found that neither the total scope of interpersonal contact with Indians nor specific forms of contact had any systematic impact upon the perceptions of Indians held by our respondents. For example, the frequency with which specific types of differences or problems were mentioned by respondents with limited or no interpersonal contact was virtually identical to that reported by respondents with a broader range of contact. Similarly, experience with specific forms of contact did not appear to affect the frequency with which differences between Indians and non-Indians, or Indian problems, were mentioned.[7]

In the light of these rather surprising findings, we pursued two other dimensions of interpersonal contact. The sociological literature on the effects of black–white contact in the United States indicates that whites' attitudes toward blacks are affected by whether or not the cross-racial contact involves persons of equal status and whether or not the contact involved pleasant or unpleasant experiences. However, when we asked those of our respondents who had experienced contact with Indians at work whether the respondent's job was "better than, about the same as, or worse than the job held by the Indian," we found that this dimension of contact had no bearing upon how respondents perceived Indians. Secondly, perceptions seemed unaffected by whether or not the interpersonal contact was pleasant or unpleasant in character.

Not only did this latter dimension of contact yield very few statistically significant differences when related to perceptions of Indians, but when those differences did exist, they tended to be of a rather surprising nature. For instance, on both the question involving differences between Indians and other Canadians and the question involving the main problems faced by Canadian Indians today, respondents who reported having had only pleasant experiences with Indians were the most likely to cite personality deficiencies on the part of Indians. Similarly, those respondents who had had only pleasant experiences with Indians were the most likely to cite the use of alcohol as a difference between Indians and other Canadians. Thus we are led to conclude that it is not the mere fact of having had or not having had a pleasant or unpleasant experience with Indians that influences perceptions of Indians. Rather, it is more likely the specific circumstances of those encounters, and the significance attached to them by the non-Indian person, which influences non-Indians' perceptions of Indians.

To summarize, contact was found to have virtually no impact upon perceptions. This is probably due to three factors: (1) our lack of more detailed information on the contact situations (e.g. recentness, frequency, duration, and significance to the respondent); (2) respondents over-reporting their contact with Indians[8]; and (3) the fact that increased scope of contact leads to an increased likelihood of having *both* pleasant and unpleasant experiences with Indians.

GENERALIZED SYMPATHY TOWARDS INDIANS AND INDIAN CONCERNS

Our discussion to this point has not addressed a number of critical questions. For instance, what, overall, is the disposition of Prairie sentiments towards Indians? Are Western Canadians sympathetic or unsympathetic towards the conditions, treatment, and aspirations of Indians? Are Western Canadians polarized into "liberal" and "illiberal" camps, or are they beset by ambivalence or indifference?

To address these questions we must momentarily move away from specific perceptions and seek a more general measure of public dispositions. Our tool in this respect is an *Indian Sympathy Index* which aggregates the reactions of individuals to ten different agree–disagree·statements encompassing a wide variety of Indian issues. As the composition and construction of the Sympathy Index have been discussed elsewhere,[9] we shall simply note here that total index scores could potentially range from ten (which would reflect a very unsympathetic response to each of the ten agree–disagree statements) to fifty (which would reflect a very sympathetic response to each statement).[10] Figure 1 presents the distribution of index scores for both the Prairie sample and the non-Prairie national sample.

Figure 1 clearly illustrates that Prairie sentiment toward Indians and Indian issues is not polarized into "liberal" and "illiberal" camps. Rather, it is more symmetrically distributed about the mean, with relatively few respondents being located at either extreme. Figure 1 also illustrates, however, that sentiment in the Prairie provinces is markedly less sympathetic than it is elsewhere in Canada.

The distribution of Prairie sentiment depicted in Figure 1 masks some significant interprovincial variation among the Prairie provinces.[11] Respondents in Manitoba were, on the average, considerably more sympathetic toward Indians and Indian issues than the overall Prairie distribution would suggest, while Saskatchewan respondents were significantly less so. In general, however, the differences in average provincial scores on the Sympathy Index represent the accumulation of small and usually statistically insignificant differences across the ten statements comprising the index.

We have now examined several measures of Prairie residents' perceptions of, and sentiments toward, Indians and Indian issues. However, before we turn to a discussion of some potential sources of change in Prairie sentiment, we should like to examine attitudes toward two more specific issue areas which are very important in forging the new accommodative structures which Indians are striving to establish with the non-Indian Canadian society. The first of these is land claims, which, as previously mentioned, constitute for some Indians the very foundation upon which the new accommodative structures are to be erected. The second of the two issue areas is that of the tactics which are available to Indians as they seek to drive home to bureaucrats, politicians, and others the message that new accommodative structures are desperately needed.

LAND CLAIMS

During the past decade, a large number of Indian land claims have been filed, many of which have attracted great public attention because of their scope, or their implications for resource development, or both. This is surely one of the most contentious, or potentially most contentious, issues arising between Indians and the broader society. Thus in our study we devoted considerable emphasis to the measurement of opinions toward Indian land claims.[12]

In seeking to probe respondents' perceptions of Indian motivations in making land claims, we asked the following question: "Do you feel that when Indians lay claim to land in Canada they are *mainly* interested in the land

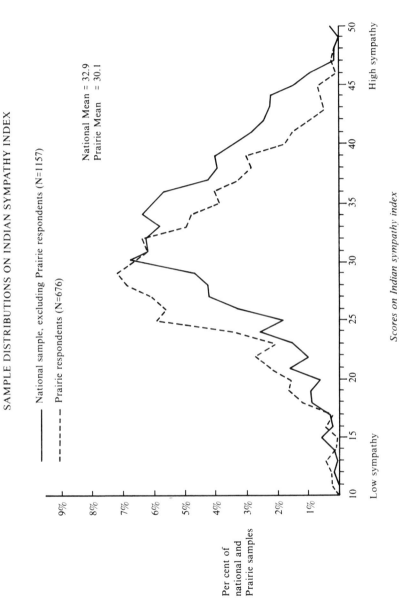

FIGURE 1

SAMPLE DISTRIBUTIONS ON INDIAN SYMPATHY INDEX

——— National sample, excluding Prairie respondents (N=1157)

------- Prairie respondents (N=676)

National Mean = 32.9
Prairie Mean = 30.1

Per cent of
national and
Prairie samples

Low sympathy

Scores on Indian sympathy index

High sympathy

for its own sake or are they mainly interested in it *for the money* it might bring?" Faced with these alternatives, 35.5 per cent of the sample felt that Indians were interested in the money that the land might bring, and 25.2 per cent perceived both motives in land claims. Interestingly, Albertans were the most likely to perceive a pecuniary interest in land claims, compelling one to speculate that the capitalist ethic may well enjoy a more robust existence in Alberta than elsewhere in the Prairies. In this regard, though, it should be noted that we have no evidence that pecuniary motives are considered to be any less valid, legitimate, or desirable by respondents than are other motives.

The question reported in Table 3 moves away from the motivations underlying land claims to a more central concern—the perceived validity of such claims. If public opinion is to have any effect on the resolution of Indian land claims, the major impact will likely come from perceptions of legitimacy and validity, rather than from perceptions of motivation *per se.*

TABLE 3

VALIDITY OF INDIAN LAND CLAIMS*

Option Chosen	Man.	Sask.	Alta.	Total Prairies	Total Canada, Non-Prairies
A) All are valid	9.2	7.1	4.5	6.5	12.2
B) Many are valid	46.1	31.1	41.8	40.3	54.2
C) Few are valid	35.9	55.7	45.5	45.4	27.5
D) None are valid	8.8	6.1	8.2	7.8	6.1
Total (excluding non-response)	100.0%	100.0%	100.0%	100.0%	100.0%
N =	182	163	203	548	1109

Chi square significance = .01

* "Overall, do you feel that *all* Indian land claims are valid, *many* are valid, *few* are valid, or *no* Indian land claims are valid?"

On balance, the Prairie population may appear at first glance to be more unsupportive than supportive of Indian land claims. While 46.8 per cent of the Prairie sample felt that many or all Indian land claims are valid, 53.2 per cent felt that few or none are valid. Nevertheless, a substantial and perhaps even surprising degree of public support for native land claims does exist. Only 7.8 per cent felt that none of the land claims are valid, while 92.2 per cent of those with an opinion on the question granted the validity of at least some Indian land claims. We should also note from the table that support for Indian land claims is significantly higher in Manitoba than it is in Alberta or Saskatchewan.

In some respects, the question on validity is difficult to interpret because it is addressed to land claims in general, whereas specific land claims vary greatly in their magnitude, their implications for the broader society, and the degree of support or opposition that they generate within that society.[13] We thus also incorporated a question on one particular land claim, filed by Indians in northern Alberta shortly before our study, and encompassing the Athabasca oil sands.

When asked if they had heard of this claim, 61.8 per cent of our Prairie respondents replied that they had.[14] Respondents who had heard of the claim were then asked what they felt Indians were trying to accomplish with the claim: were they trying to prevent the oil sands from ever being developed, to obtain greater Indian participation in oil sands projects already underway, or to get total Indian control of the oil sands? Only a relative handful of respondents (6.1 per cent) felt that Indians were trying to block permanently development of the oil sands. A more common belief (shared by 28.2 per cent) was that Indians were trying to get total control of the oil sands. The most common perception, however, was that Indians were trying to obtain greater participation in the projects already underway at the oil sands. This belief, shared by 60.0 per cent of those Prairie respondents who had heard of the Indian claim, appears to coincide with the rationale publicized by the Indian Association of Alberta at the time it filed the claim. This publicity may also account for the finding that Alberta respondents were more likely than those in Saskatchewan or Manitoba to state greater participation as the Indian goal.

TACTICAL OPTIONS FACING CANADIAN INDIANS

Over the past decade, Canadian Indians have employed a wide variety of tactics in promoting their cause and publicizing their grievances. Not only have they frequently used such "conventional" tactics as lawsuits, but there has also been a growing emphasis on more radical tactics such as blockades, armed and unarmed occupations, and threats of violence. It was this apparent shift toward radicalism that led us to pay particular attention to the public response to tactical radicalism. We were interested in whether or not tactical radicalism might undermine levels of public support and sympathy for the Indian cause, and in whether or not radicalism might trigger some form of backlash within the non-Indian population.[15]

As we cannot discuss here all the data we collected on public reactions to Indian radicalism, we should like to focus upon one question which asked respondents to state their degree of approval or disapproval of Indians using each of seven tactical options. The question and the responses to it are reported in Table 4. There we find that requesting a Royal Commission and launching lawsuits both win majority approval, but for each of the other five tactics at least a plurality of the sample disapproved. The rate of disapproval reached a peak with "threatening violence," a tactic of which almost 96 per cent of the respondents disapproved, most of them strongly.

TABLE 4

DEGREE OF APPROVAL FOR VARIOUS TACTICAL OPTIONS FACING INDIANS*

*Per Cent of the Prairie Sample Who:***

Tactical Option***	Strongly Approve	Moderately Approve	Neither Approve nor Disapprove	Moderately Disapprove	Strongly Disapprove
1) Requesting that a Royal Commission be formed to study Indian problems	44.5	37.0	7.3	5.5	5.7
2) Launching lawsuits in the courts	21.5	40.2	14.6	10.6	13.0
3) Holding protest marches	8.2	33.8	14.8	21.1	22.1
4) Occupation of government offices	9.7	22.3	12.7	22.6	32.6
5) Boycotting private businesses	4.2	9.2	21.2	26.5	38.8
6) Barricading roads and railways crossing Indian reserves	2.6	10.0	11.7	23.6	52.0
7) Threatening violence	0.7	1.3	2.4	15.0	80.6

* "Putting aside the effectiveness or ineffectiveness of each tactic, please tell me whether you would *approve* or *disapprove* of Indians actually *using* these different tactics."

** Respondents with no opinion (1.8% to 4.3% of the sample) excluded from this table.

*** Order scrambled on questionnaire.

For the national sample excluding Prairie respondents the percentages strongly or moderately approving of each tactic are as follows:
(1) 87.6%; (2) 67.3%; (3) 60.0%; (4) 37.3%; (5) 14.7%; (6) 17.7%; (7) 2.8%.

There are several aspects of Table 4 that warrant emphasis. The first is that even for the two most innocuous tactics on the list, launching lawsuits and requesting a Royal Commission, a significant level of disapproval is found within the Prairie sample. Secondly, it is interesting to note that more people would approve of Indians occupying government offices than would approve of Indians boycotting private business. Although the former seems to be the more radical of the two tactics, it may be the case that the government, but not private business, is perceived by a substantial part of the public as a legitimate target of Indian protest. Finally, with respect to "threatening violence," not only did an overwhelming percentage of the sample disapprove, but few people expressed indifference.

The potential for outbreaks of violence in Indian protest, and the serious consequences that such outbreaks could have on non-Indian public opinion (and subsequently upon Indians themselves) led us to include another question on violence in the interview. Thus, the following question was posed to respondents:

Some people say that no good can *ever* come from Indians using violence. Other people say that violence is justified under *certain* circumstances. What is your opinion—would you say that violence by Indians is justified under *no* circumstances, for self-defence only, or when all other means of getting their message across have failed?

For the total Prairie sample, 41.9 per cent replied "under no circumstances," 45.1 per cent said "for self-defence only," 10.7 per cent said "when all other means have failed."

The response to this question suggests a higher acceptance of violence than was implied by the 2.0 per cent of the sample in Table 4 which approved "threatening violence." The level of support, however, is still minimal. In general, the reaction of Prairie respondents to tactical radicalism suggests that the employment by Indians of radical tactics may seriously compromise pre-existing levels of public support and sympathy. However, the actual outcome of violence with respect to non-Indian public opinion would depend, no doubt, on the circumstances surrounding the event and upon the manner in which the event was both portrayed in the media and characterized by public officials. Furthermore, our research provides no insight as to whether the potential gains of radicalism, both with respect to mobilizing the native community and jolting the government into action, might outweigh the potential costs in public support.[16] Our research simply suggests that such potential costs exist and that their magnitude may be considerable.

SOURCES OF CHANGE IN PRAIRIE SENTIMENT

Our survey offers a snapshot of Prairie residents' perceptions of Canadian Indians, a snapshot taken during the early months of 1976. We cannot assume, however, that the perceptions we have described are static. On the contrary, we must assume that such perceptions are always open to change. As new events, issues, demands, and leaders emerge, public opinion will inevitably be affected, but, of course, the degree to which existing opinions will change, and the direction in which they will change, cannot be determined until the character of future events unfolds.

There are other potential sources of change, however, that can be examined through our survey. These sources lie within the process of social and demographic change which moves inexorably through the Prairie population. For example, over time, the population of Western Canada is being exposed to greater and greater formal education; a child born today can expect, on the average, to spend more years undergoing formal education than did his parents. Secondly, the composition of the population is changing as older members die and are replaced. The population, in effect, is undergoing continual generational change. It is the implications that these two sources of change have for Prairie residents' perceptions of Canada's native peoples to which we now turn.

Educational Change

The principal relevance of educational change to our present research lies in the frequently observed relationship between levels of formal education and inter-group attitudes. Specifically, studies have found that individuals with relatively advanced formal educations generally emerge as more "liberal" in their orientations toward inter-group relations and minority group demands than do those individuals with less extensive education. Hence, if it can be shown in this instance that levels of formal education are related to the perceptions of native Canadians held by Prairie respondents, then we can at least speculate on what continued educational change within the Prairie population might entail for attitudes toward the conditions, concerns, and aspirations of Canadian Indians, all other conditions being equal.

If we return first to the question on major differences between Canadian Indians and other Canadians, we find that, in some respects, the four educational groups shown in Table 5 vary quite sharply in the types of differences they reported.[17] Table 5 presents the four categories where statistically significant differences exist among the four educational groups. Thus we find that those respondents with relatively high levels of formal education were much more inclined than were those respondents with limited educations to cite differences related to poverty and culture. On the other hand, alcohol-related differences were cited much more frequently by respondents with relatively limited formal educations.

In general, levels of formal education also tend to have a substantial impact upon the types of problems perceived to be faced by Canadian Indians today, as statistically significant differences once again emerge across the four educational subgroups. Specifically, as Table 6 shows, respondents

TABLE 5

MAJOR DIFFERENCES BETWEEN CANADIAN INDIANS AND OTHER CANADIANS
BY EDUCATION OF RESPONDENT

PERCENTAGE MENTIONING TYPE OF DIFFERENCE

Education of Respondent

Type of Difference	Grade School	High School	Some Post Secondary	University Degree
	N = 123	N = 354	N = 123	N = 74
1) Poverty or poor living conditions of Indians*	3.7	11.5	17.2	24.2
2) Differences in the use of alcohol*	16.9	7.5	5.6	0.0
3) Discrimination and/or prejudice*	5.3	18.6	21.4	8.3
4) Differences in culture, heritage and lifestyle*	15.8	14.6	25.8	27.6

* Analysis of variance significant at .01 or better.

with higher levels of education were more likely than those with lower levels of education to mention the problems of prejudice and discrimination faced by Indians and the problems of assimilation and adjustment. However, persons with low levels of formal education were more likely than persons with higher levels of education to mention drinking or alcoholism as a problem. This is consistent with our findings on the previous question dealing with the main differences between Indians and other Canadians.

TABLE 6

MAIN PROBLEMS FACED BY CANADIAN INDIANS TODAY
BY EDUCATION OF RESPONDENT

PERCENTAGE MENTIONING TYPE OF PROBLEM

Education of Respondent

Problem Mentioned	Grade School	High School	Some Post Secondary	University Degree
	N = 123	N = 354	N = 123	N = 74
1) Drinking and/or alcoholism*	45.8	27.2	21.2	21.8
2) Prejudice and/or discrimination against Indians*	19.3	30.5	37.0	41.2
3) Problems of assimilation and adjustment*	10.7	15.8	21.6	28.6

* Analysis of variance significant at .01 or better.

Levels of formal education also had an impact on other variables examined in this study. For instance, there was a weak but statistically significant tendency for those with higher levels of formal education to be more likely to perceive Indian land claims as being valid (r = .10; p = .004). Whereas 60.7 per cent of those Prairie respondents with university degress felt that all or many Indian land claims are valid, only 34.7 per cent of those Prairie respondents with a grade school education or less felt so.

With regard to Indians' usage of specific tactics, the higher the respondents' level of formal education, the more likely he or she was to approve of Indians boycotting private businesses, holding protest marches, launching lawsuits, and requesting the formation of a Royal Commission to study Indian problems.[18] Levels of formal education, however, were statistically unrelated to approval or disapproval of Indians barricading roads or railways crossing Indian reserves, occupying government offices, or threatening violence.

Finally, there was a very weak relationship between levels of formal education and scores on the Indian Sympathy Index.[19] In general, respondents with relatively advanced formal educations received higher sympathy scores than did respondents with relatively little formal education.

In summary, there is substantial evidence that levels of formal education have a significant impact on Prairie residents' perceptions of native peoples, their concerns and aspirations. In general, the impact of education is liberal in direction: relatively well-educated respondents seem disproportionately supportive of Indian concerns, and even more strikingly, appear less likely to hold what would appear to be negative ethnic "stereotypes." Thus we might expect that, as educational advances continue to be made across the Canadian West, their effect will be to intensify support for native peoples within the non-Indian Prairie population.

Age and Generational Change

Societies continually replace themselves as their members are thinned out by death and replenished by birth. As this process takes place, the young take on many of the beliefs, values, and social institutions of their predecessors. The transferral is less than perfect, however, as historical circumstances vary across generations. For example, people who are today in their late twenties and thirties came to maturity during the American civil rights movement, a period in which prevailing social attitudes toward minorities were undergoing radical revision. Thus, in the wake of the dramatic social change that has occurred within North America in the past two decades, the prospects of intergenerational stability in cross-group perceptions and attitudes seem unlikely.

Our concern here is with whether or not substantial differences exist among Prairie residents of different ages in their perceptions of native peoples. If we turn first to the question asked about major differences between native Canadian Indians and other Canadians, we find no systematic or linear age trends in public perceptions. Secondly, on the question concerning the main problems faced by contemporary Canadian Indians, significant age differences existed in two instances only: the mention of prejudice and discrimination as a problem declined sharply with age; and the mention of alcohol related problems rose with age.

Substantial age differences were found in the questions relating to Indian land claims, with older respondents being more likely to feel that Indians sought money through the land claims, and being more likely to reject the validity of Indian land claims.[20]

Older respondents were also less likely than younger respondents to approve of Indians using the first six of the seven tactics listed in Table 4. The relationship was particularly striking for reactions to Indian occupations of government offices, a tactic of which 49.5 per cent of respondents aged eighteen to twenty-nine would approve, contrasted to only 17.3 per cent of respondents fifty-five and over.

In general, we have witnessed substantial age effects across the questions explored in this paper. Younger respondents have displayed somewhat different perceptions of Indian problems and differences, have been more supportive of Indian land claims, and would be more willing to approve most means that Indians might utilize to press their grievances and claims upon the broader society. One last finding, however, must temper any conclusion that generational change will lead to a more supportive public climate in the Prairies for Indian concerns. This last finding concerns the Indian Sympathy Index, where we found no trend for sympathy to increase among younger Prairie respondents.[21] In this case, then, there was no evidence to support a liberalization of Prairie sentiment among the young, although here, as in all the previous questions, there was no evidence of any growing or disproportionate hostility among young Western Canadians.

CONCLUSIONS

That the accommodative structures erected a century ago are breaking down seems indisputable. Our data on the attitudes of non-Indians towards Indians suggest that present public opinion is receptive to Indians working out new accommodations with Canadian society. In fact, these data also suggest that if the process of socio-political change were to unfold smoothly without a national political crisis, the climate of opinion might well be even more conducive to Indian desires in another fifteen years, although we are in no way suggesting that Indians should postpone until then their political and legal efforts to reach a new accommodation with Canadian society. Indeed new accommodations are already emerging, as can be seen in the facts that Indians now have regular access to the federal cabinet, concrete proposals for a revised Indian Act have been formulated,[22] partnerships are being proposed between Indians and private business and between poor and wealthy Indian bands, land claims are being negotiated and settled, churches have dramatically altered their previous stance,[23] and Indian leaders may finally be assuming positions of major responsibility in the bureaucracy which in the past has been a major source of frustration to them.

However, Grimshaw's contention[24] that accommodative structures are inherently unstable will probably hold true for the accommodations cited above and for others yet to emerge, regardless of whether or not they are implemented in an atmosphere of Indian–government consensus. If such accommodations are imposed upon the natives (for example, through the extinguishment of aboriginal land titles or in the face of disagreement amongst the Indians themselves), the underlying conflict which gave rise to the need to revise the prior accommodations in the first instance will only have been regulated, rather than resolved. That conflict presumably will retain the potential for breaking forth again during some period in the near or distant future when the governing non-Indian regime is weak.[25] However, if a more "enlightened" stance is adopted by government such that new accommodations come closer to being based on a consensus, the potential for future conflict is lessened,[26] although the need for new accommodative structures will reappear periodically as society continues to modernize and old accommodations are no longer useful or efficient. While this latter point should be obvious in light of the repeated adjustments which have had to be made to the Canadian federal system to accommodate the English and the French, public opinion pressures might nevertheless arise for a permanent "solution" to "the Indian problem,"[27] just as pressures have arisen in English Canada to "get the Quebec problem settled once and forever."

The challenge for government leaders will be to resist such ill-informed and unrealistic pressures. Canadians and their leaders must come to realize that colonialism is inherently a dialectical phenomenon the legacy of which is a set of extremely difficult and ever-changing problems and conflicts in the relationships between the colonizers and the colonized. Attempts at assimilation, whether forced or voluntary, fly in the face of this dialectical fact of life, while the only other permanent solutions—expulsion or genocide—are obviously not viable either. Thus, in light both of the inherently conflict-ridden nature of Indian–non-Indian relations and of the relentless nature of social change in modern society, no permanent solutions can be attained. The best that we can expect is a series of temporary, but forward-looking and mutually agreeable, accommodations which stem from a negotiation process in which the gross imbalance in negotiating power between Indians and government has been rectified to the fullest reasonable extent.

Notes

[1]See Alan Grimshaw, "Interpreting Collective Violence: An Argument for the Importance of Social Structure," in *Collective Violence*, ed. James Short and Marvin Wolfgang (Chicago: Aldine Atherton, 1972), pp. 35–46.

[2]The urban migration of Canadian Indians has been examined in Edgar Dosman, *Indians: The Urban Dilemma* (Toronto: McClelland and Stewart, 1972); Mark Nagler, *Indians in the City* (Ottawa: Canadian Research Centre for Anthropology, 1970); and W. T. Stanbury, *Success and Failure: Indians in Urban Society* (Vancouver: University of British Columbia Press, 1975).

[3]See E. Palmer Patterson II, *The Canadian Indian: A History Since 1500* (Don Mills, Ont.: Collier-Macmillan, 1972).

[4]It was only in this case that significant interprovincial variation was encountered, with 29.1 per cent of the Alberta respondents mentioning education-related problems, compared to only 18.6 per cent of the Saskatchewan and 19.9 per cent of the Manitoba respondents.

[5]Marlene Mackie, "Ethnic Stereotypes and Prejudice: Alberta Indians, Hutterites, and Ukrainians," *Canadian Ethnic Studies* 6 (1974): 39–52.

[6]See especially Robin Williams, "Race and Ethnic Relations," *Annual Review of Sociology* 1 (1975): 125–64.

[7]Relatively minor and statistically weak exceptions were encountered with contact through organizations and clubs.

[8]For instance, we are sceptical of the fact that 40 per cent of the Prairie sample reported having had a close Indian friend and 57 per cent reported having had a neighbour who is an Indian. These figures may reflect a "social desirability" bias.

[9]See Roger Gibbins and J. Rick Ponting, "Contemporary Prairie Perceptions of Canada's Native Peoples, *Prairie Forum* 2, no. 1 (1977): 57–81.

[10]The actual range in the Prairie sample was from eleven to forty-eight.

[11]The analysis of variance for inter-provincial variation on the Sympathy Index was significant at the .001 level of confidence.

[12]The interview explored several aspects of Indian land claims upon which we do not report in this paper. For additional details, see Roger Gibbins and J. Rick Ponting, "Public Perceptions of Native Land Claims: A Preliminary Report" (Paper presented to the Annual Meeting of the Canadian Sociology and Anthropology Association, Quebec City, Quebec, 1976).

[13]For a discussion of this, see the paper by the Indian claims commissioner, Lloyd Barber, "The Nature of Indian Claims" (Presented to the Conference on Culture, Education, and Ethnic Canadians, Regina, Saskatchewan, 1976).

[14]As we should expect, Albertans were the most likely to have heard of the oil sands claim. In the Alberta sub-sample, 76.6 per cent of the respondents had heard of the claim, compared to 51.6 per cent in Saskatchewan and 46.0 per cent in Manitoba.

[15]For a more detailed discussion of these issues, see J. Rick Ponting and Roger Gibbins, "English Canadians' and French Quebecers' Reactions to Contemporary Indian Protest" (Paper presented to the Ninth World Congress of Sociology, Uppsala, Sweden, 1978).

[16]For further discussion of this trade-off, see Roger Gibbins and J. Rick Ponting, "Public Opinion and Canadian Indians: A Preliminary Probe" *Canadian Ethnic Studies* 8, no. 2 (1977): 1–17.

[17]Respondents with higher levels of formal education were statistically significantly more likely than those with lower levels of formal education to cite at least one difference between Indians

and non-Indians. This low response rate among persons with a grade school education may reflect a low level of articulateness in handling open-ended questions.

[18]The Pearson correlation coefficients between approval and the respondent's level of formal education were as follows: holding protest marches (r. = .17, sig. = .001), requesting the formation of a Royal Commission (r = .11, sig. = .002), boycotting private businesses (r = .20, sig. = .001), and launching lawsuits (r = .18, sig. = .001).

[19]The Pearson correlation between index scores and levels of formal education was .09, significant at the .009 level of confidence. However, a one-way analysis of variance for index scores across the four educational subsamples was statistically insignificant even at the .05 level of confidence.

[20]While 57.2 per cent of the youngest respondents felt that "all" or "many" Indian land claims are valid, this proportion fell steadily until it reached only 33.4 per cent for the oldest respondents.

[21]The Pearson correlation between age and the Indian Sympathy Index was insignificant (r = .05, sig. = .085), as was the one-way analysis of variance among the four age categories (significance = .310).

[22]See, for example, Harold Cardinal, *The Rebirth of Canada's Indians* (Edmonton: Hurtig, 1977).

[23]See Hugh McCullum and Carmel McCullum, *This Land Is Not for Sale* (Toronto: Anglican Book Centre, 1975).

[24]Grimshaw, "Interpreting Collective Violence."

[25]Such an outbreak of conflict between Indians and the non-Indian government, is only likely to be avoided if Indians are given a vested interest in the new accommodative structures. Since such vested interests are unlikely to be evenly distributed throughout Indian society, the end result under such a "solution" might simply be to displace the conflict from the Indian–government plane onto the inter-Indian plane. This, of course, is simply a form of the "divide and rule" strategy, and does not eliminate conflict.

[26]See Ali Mazrui, "Pluralism and National Integration," in *Pluralism in Africa*, ed. Leo Kuper and M. G. Smith (Los Angeles and Berkeley: University of California Press, 1971), pp. 333–49, for a discussion of the phenomenon whereby a history of successfully resolving intergroup conflicts increases the degree of integration of the groups involved.

[27]Our study was not designed to detect any such public opinion pressures, and we accordingly did not discover any. However, the sociological literature on "bystander publics" (Ralph Turner and Lewis M. Killian, *Collective Behaviour*, 2nd ed. [Englewood Cliffs, N.J.: Prentice-Hall, 1972], pp. 238–39) suggests that such pressures will soon emerge.

8

The Canadian Government's Termination Policy:
From 1969 to the Present Day

MARIE SMALLFACE MARULE

The policy of assimilation of the Indians into the Euro-Canadian society has been the Indian policy of every government of Canada since Confederation. It is the result of the historical relations that evolved between the Indians of Canada and the colonial governments prior to Confederation.[1] It is also the result of centuries of misunderstandings due to the Euro-Canadian racist assumptions that the Indian race and culture are inferior and that the "superior race," out of a sense of duty and generosity, must civilize the "savage" and assimilate him into the dominant society. The objectives of this policy have been "civilization" of the Indian and termination of any special status for Indians and Indian lands. Through time, these objectives have remained the same, being modified only by the emphasis placed on them by different administrations. The methods of different administrations have varied, and have been complicated by conflicts of interest, political expediency, and good intentions.[2] The focal point of government policy has remained the "reserve"—that is, "the tract of land, the legal title to which is vested in Her Majesty, that has been set apart by Her Majesty for the use and benefit of a band."[3] And the primary concern of the successive administrations has been to limit the cost of the necessary programmes.[4]

An examination of the "Statement of the Government of Canada on Indian Policy, 1969,"[5] better known as the White Paper, with reference to some of the activities of the Department of Indian Affairs since 1969, together with circulated government policy directives on local government and post-secondary education for Indians, will show that the objectives and methods for their achievement are still rooted in the past history of Indian–government relations. It is clear that government policy is still directed toward assimilation of the Indians of Canada; cost is still a primary concern.

THE 1969 WHITE PAPER

In June 1969 the Honourable Jean Chrétien, minister of Indian affairs and northern development, presented to the first session of the twenty-eighth Parliament a proposed "new" Indian Policy on behalf of the Liberal government. Essentially, the "new policy" was to provide Indians with "the right to full and equal participation in the cultural, social, economic and political life of Canada." The framework within which this goal could be achieved required:

(1) That the legislative and constitutional bases of discrimination be removed; (2) that there be positive recognition by everyone of the unique contribution of Indian culture to Canadian life; (3) that services come through the same channels and from the same government agencies for all Canadians; (4) that those who are furthest behind be helped most; (5) that lawful obligations be recognized; (6) that control of Indian land be transferred to the Indian people.[6]

To create this necessary framework, the government was prepared to take the following steps:

(1) Propose to Parliament that the Indian Act be repealed and take such legislative steps as be necessary to enable Indians to control Indian lands and to acquire title to them. (2) Propose to the Governments of the Provinces that they take over the same responsibility for Indians that they have for other citizens in their provinces. The take-over would be accomplished by the transfer to the provinces of federal funds normally provided for Indian programs, augmented as may be necessary. (3) Make substantial funds available for Indian economic development as an interim measure. (4) Wind up that part of the Department of Indian Affairs and Northern Development which deals with Indian Affairs. The residual responsibilities would be transferred to other appropriate federal departments. In addition, the Government will appoint a Commissioner to consult with the Indians and to study and recommend acceptable procedures for the adjudication of claims.[7]

Contrary to the minister's suggestion that his "new" policy would "change longstanding policies" which did not "serve the interest of either the Indian people or their fellow Canadians,"[8] an examination of the history of Indian policy in Canada shows the same policy has long been in effect. John Tobias has researched the roots of Canada's Indian policy and states that it is based on the colonial goal "to remove all legal distinctions between Indians and other Canadians, and integrate them fully into Canadian society."[9] The policy of assimilation was reflected in the intention of the legislation of 1857 when the united colonies of Upper and Lower Canada passed "an Act to encourage the gradual civilization of the Indians in this Province." This law is the foundation for the present Indian Act and reserve system.

Following Confederation, the policy of assimilation was officially sanctioned in 1869 by the government of Sir John A. Macdonald through the passage of "an Act for the gradual enfranchisement of Indians." The intention to "take such legislative steps as may be necessary to enable Indians . . . to acquire title to [Indian lands]"[10] was also the purpose of the first Indian Act when it was passed in 1876 as part of this former "new" policy. The legislation of 1876 stipulated, according to John Tobias,

> that the Superintendent General have the reserve surveyed into individual lots. The band council could then assign these lots to individual band members. As a form of title, the Superintendent General would then give the band member a location ticket. Before an individual received a ticket, he had to prove he was "civilized" in the same manner as under the earlier legislation.[11] On passing this first test, and receiving his location ticket, the Indian entered a three-year probationary period during which he had to demonstrate that he would use the land as a Euro-Canadian might and that he was fully qualified for a membership in Canadian society. If he passed these tests, he was enfranchised and given title to his land. If all band members wished, they could enfranchise in this way.[12]

When this did not result in immediate attempts by many Indians to enfranchise, amounting to less than 250 cases in sixty-three years, the government passed legislation authorizing enforced enfranchisement in 1920.[13]

The issue of Indian title to Indian land exemplifies one of the major misunderstandings between the Indian people and the governments of Canada. Since the establishment of the reserve system, governments of Canada, colonial and confederate, have viewed the protection of Indian lands from alienation as a transitional measure to be terminated at some opportune time in favour of Indian ownership and use of land under the Canadian land tenure system of individual fee simple title, subject to the Canadian tax structure.[14] This position is clearly reflected in the 1969 White Paper:

> The Government believes that full ownership implies many things. It carries with it the free choice of use, of retention or of disposition. In

our society it also carries with it an obligation to pay for certain services. The Government recognizes that it may not be acceptable to put all lands into the provincial systems immediately and make them subject to taxes. When the Indian people see that the only way they can own and fully control land is to accept taxation the way other Canadians do, they will make that decision.

On the other hand, the Indians signed the treaties with the British Crown believing they were securing for themselves portions of their original territories for their exclusive use as homelands on which they may continue their existence as a people, adapting at their own pace to their changing environment with the assistance and support promised by the government agents in return for their agreement to allow European use of their remaining territories. It was their understanding that the government undertook the responsibilities to protect their homelands from encroachment and alienation. They never perceived the need or requirement to govern themselves and their homelands in accordance with European customs. This is made evident by the failure of the Indian Act provisions for enfranchisement and the resistance to the Indian Act regulations and requirements for local governments.[15]

It is revealing to note that one hundred years ago (1877) when Treaty Seven was being negotiated with the Indian tribes of Southern Alberta, the government had already established the policy of assimilation, and through its institutionalized reserve system, assumed legislative control over Indian lands.[16] The acts of 1869 and 1876 were already being applied to Indians in Eastern Canada.[17]

The issue of protection of Indian lands from alienation by seizure for failure to pay taxes is also relevant to the issue of federal jurisdiction and responsibility for Indians and Indian lands. In the 1969 White Paper, the federal government argued that the provinces should assume the responsibilities for Indians within their provincial boundaries. It proposed to negotiate "with the provinces [to] conclude agreements under which Indian people would participate in and be serviced by the full programs of the provincial and local systems."[18] The agreements negotiated would determine a cost-sharing formula prescribed by the federal budget for the Indian programmes in each province and based on the principle that such provisions would eventually decrease. The provinces ultimately would assume full responsibility for Indian residents in their boundaries the same as for other citizens. The inevitability of Indian taxation upon provincial assumption of full responsibility was put in the context that Indians, to receive the right to treatment as full citizens in the provinces, must be prepared to accept the responsibilities that go with that privilege.[19]

The irony with respect to the proposed transfer of responsibilities to the provinces is that it was already proposed in 1947 by the Joint Committee of the Senate and House of Commons on Indian Affairs and acted upon in the 1950's, with the result that provincial governments were delivering education and health services to Indians well before the 1969 proposal was presented to Parliament.[20] It should be noted that the cost for the provincial service for Indians was far above that for the other citizens of a province, and neither the provinces nor the Indians wished to have jurisdiction and responsibility transferred from the federal government to the provincial governments.

The foregoing examination of some of the proposals outlined in the 1969 White Paper has attempted to indicate that many of the methods proposed by the present Liberal government vary little from those of previous administrations and that the objectives and the goals remain the same.

The following examination of some specific developments in the area of Indian affairs since 1969 will show that the policy of assimilation is still in effect. Furthermore, contrary to the assurances of the federal government in June 1970 that it would withdraw its White Paper, the proposals of 1969 are still being implemented.

DUPLICITY, SUBTERFUGE, AND TERMINATION STRATEGY

The most revealing evidence that implementation of the 1969 policy is proceeding with government initiative is the following passage from a letter written to the prime minister, Pierre Trudeau, by the minister of Indian affairs and northern development, the Honourable Jean Chrétien, in 1971:

In essence, then, we are deliberately furthering an evolutionary process of provincial and Indian inter-involvement by promoting contacts at every opportunity at all levels of government, at the same time recognizing the truth of the matter—that progress will take place in different areas in different ways at a different pace. Experience shows that the reference to a time frame in the policy of 1969 was one of the prime targets of those who voiced the Indian opposition to the proposals. The course upon which we are now embarked seems to present a more promising approach to the long term objectives than might be obtained by setting specific deadlines for relinquishing federal administration.[21]

In the area of Indian economic development, a fund was established in 1969—a direct result of the white paper proposal to "make substantial additional funds available for *investment* [italics added] in the economic progress of the Indian people."[22] The fund *was* a means for government investment in the economic progress of the Indian people, since it was primarily a loan fund available at conventional rates of interest.[23] Prerequisites for its use required incorporation of the business and a lease surrender for the reserve land on which the business would be situated. The regulations requiring incorporation had the effect of furthering assimilation by imposing a European system of ownership and control. The land lease requirement brought in provincial taxation, and use of reserve land as collateral opened the door to the possibility of expropriation. The fund had no value for the impoverished band requiring financial support for social and economic development.[24] Despite the government's pronouncement that "those who are furthest behind be helped most,"[25] it had the effect of helping wealthier individuals to develop Indian entrepreneurship.

Then, in 1970, in response to the desperate housing shortages on reserves, the Department of Indian Affairs proposed to transfer financial responsibility for housing to the Central Mortgage and Housing Corporation (C.M.H.C.) as part of the government's avowed intention to utilize all available resources to provide "enriched services to the needy Indian areas."[26] Again, this proposal had a dual purpose—to further assimilation and to make the Indian pay for it. In essence, the C.M.H.C. would provide mortgage monies to incorporated band authorities to provide the needed housing, subject to the authority having the land as collateral and the authorization to secure band funds for repayment of mortgages.[27] The greatest need for housing was, however, in the most impoverished areas with little economic potential without the necessary capital funds. Again, it was the wealthy communities which could utilize this programme, but only at great risk to their land and funds held in trust by the Department of Indian Affairs.

Recommendations put forward for departmental action by the Department of Indian Affairs regional and headquarters directors at their conference in Kingston in November 1974 eliminate any doubt that the department has been implementing the proposals put forward in 1969. To quote some of their recommendations:

1. Terminate the noon-day lunch supplement on June 30, 1975.
2. Increase the number of Indian para-professional counsellors and decrease the number of professional education counsellors.
3. Where provincial loans and grants are available to Indian students, direct Indians to this source as a first resort.
4. Consider the use of more Submissions to Cabinet so that its members will be aware of the problems, particularly on such things as off-reserve services, responsibilities of the provinces for services, five-year review of funding of association, etc.

5. Review with the Solicitor General policing on reserves with a view to transferring it to them by April 1, 1976.
6. Study methods of phasing out the provision of I.E.A. services to off-reserve Indians and determine what transitional programs the Department should provide.
7. Continue study of formula for reducing departmental funding for Bands with funds of their own.
8. Close 17 student residences over the next five years giving sufficient lead time so staffing problems will be minimized. Demolish buildings where practical alternate uses cannot be found.
9. Discuss with Mr. Hunt the transfer of I.E.A. program budget in the Yukon to the Territorial Government.[28]

In the spring of 1975, a series of departmental programme circulars concerning Indian local governments emerged. These became known as the "Local Government Guidelines, D-1 to D-5."[29] Ostensibly to further Indian self-government and self-determination through the transfer of federal programmes to bands, their effect was to impose more incorporated Indian authorities, reduce programme funding to bands, and add the threat of federal withdrawal from programme responsibility. The bands could control programme funds only if they agreed to assign their powers to a Euro-Canadian institution. The programme had to operate under these terms and conditions set by Indian affairs officials, and accept hidden overhead administrative costs and yearly funding negotiations.[30]

These guidelines had the diabolical design intended to result in one of two possible responses from the bands: (1) Frustrated with the constraints and limitations of this form of reserve "control of programmes," bands will expend more and more of their meagre resources to augment federal programmes or seek alternate sources for programme funding, thus accepting federal limitations for and/or withdrawal from programmes, or (2) Failing to deliver an effective programme due to inadequate financial support and bureaucratic interference, bands must request the Department of Indian Affairs to resume programme delivery. In this way, the civil servants and government might achieve their objectives, and they could rationalize the wisdom of their approach to Indian self-government.

On the one hand, some bands are managing their own affairs with minimal financial support, thus demonstrating the approach's success. On the other hand, Bands deemed unready for self-government provide continued justification for the department and its nine thousand civil servants. This approach has the added feature of appearing to demonstrate to Indian leaders and their communities who have had to return programme administration to the Department of Indian Affairs that they are not yet competent to govern themselves and that they should no longer criticize Indian affairs officials for poor services since they themselves failed to improve upon the services when given the opportunity to do so.

The local government guidelines, the Indian Economic Development Fund, and the Central Mortgage and Housing Corporation Indian housing programme, are deliberate vehicles for implementation of the 1969 White Paper. Most objectionable is the failure of these schemes to rectify very critical situations while serving primarily, through their terms of reference, to force acceptance of the odious policy of assimilation even though it has been rejected time and time again during the past few centuries. These programmes imposed by government officials are not only undemocratic, but also they deprive Indian people and communities of rights granted other citizens and communities in Canada. This ill-treatment of the Indians of Canada, disguised as a "solution to the Indian problem," is even more reprehensible when one considers the fact that the same treatment of Indian tribes in the United States of America had disastrous consequences for the people concerned and that the results are known to the policy makers using these methods in Canada.

The programmes and guidelines force band councils to establish Euro-Canadian institutions through which adoption of municipal government status and provincial jurisdiction is introduced on a piecemeal basis. In turn, this results in the termination of Indian rights and status by gradually undermining federal jurisdiction. This approach to termination of Indian status is essentially the same as the termination policy of the government of the United States in 1954 which resulted in disastrous consequences.[31] It only differs in application: whereas the United States policy was applied comprehensively, the Canadian approach is piecemeal. Though the rate of implementation may differ, the results will undoubtedly be the same—the loss of Indian reserve lands and the erosion of special treaty rights.

Research has been done on the effects of termination upon the Menominee tribe of Wisconsin by the well-known anthropologist, Nancy Oestreich Lurie:

Termination policy, touted as "freeing" the Indians, as applied in 1954 to the Menominee of northeastern Wisconsin, has impoverished a tribe that once paid for most of its own services and administration and has resulted in less self-determination than the Menominee exercised under the Bureau of Indian Affairs. The shift from federal to state jurisdiction, implemented between 1954 and 1961, turned the former reservation into Menominee County and turned management of the tribe's land, forests, mill and other assets over to a corporation, Menominee Enterprises, Inc., (MEI), which became virtually the only taxpayer in the new county. A situation with all the elements of classic colonialism

Plate 19. Father Albert Lacombe, O.M.I.,
who came to the Northwest in 1852,
with Blackfoot Indians, Crowfoot,
left, and Three Bulls, 1886.

Plate 20. In front, Paul Little Walker, lay-
reader at Blackfoot mission, ca.
1900.

Plate 21. Old Sun's boarding school, Anglican mission, Blackfoot Reserve, ca. 1900.

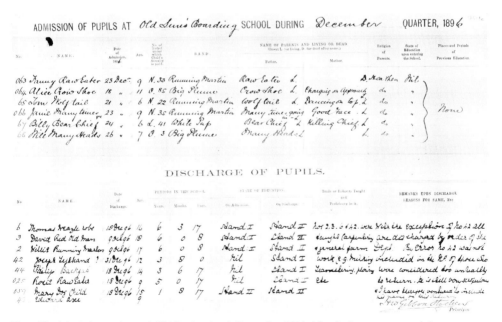

Plate 22. Admission register of Old Sun's school, December 1896. Marginal comments at right express concern about the health of some students.

Plate 23. Woodwork class at the School of Agriculture, Olds, Alberta, 1956.

Plate 24. Girls' sewing room, Industrial School, High River, Alberta, ca. 1890.

Plate 25. Treaty Seven chiefs on a visit to Ottawa, 1886.

Left to right—Back row: Father Lacombe; Jean L'Heureux. *Middle*: Three Bulls, Blackfoot; Crowfoot, Blackfoot; Red Crow, Blood. *Front*: North Axe, North Peigan; One Spot, Blood.

Plate 26. Blood Indians listening to proposals for surrendering part of their reserve, 1917. The vote favoured surrender by a small margin, but it was set aside because of fraud and bribery charges.

Plate 27. Government officials and accused photographed during trial after the Riel Rebellion, July–August 1885. Horse Child and Big Bear are to the left, Poundmaker to the right, of the front row.

Plate 28. First meeting of the League of Indians of Alberta, Duffield, 1933.

Plate 29. Royal visit to Calgary, 1939. Duck Chief, head chief of the Blackfoot, is to the right of Queen Elizabeth.

Plate 30. Senator James Gladstone, Blood Indian. Portrait taken on the occasion of his appointment to the Senate in 1958.

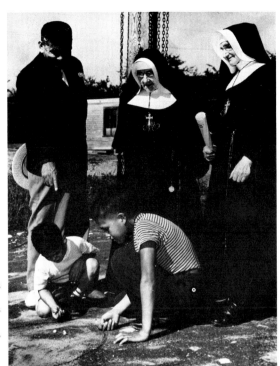

Plate 31. Andrew Paull, in 1949, with Sisters Mary Joannes and Hieronymie (on right), two of the original nuns to come from the convent of the Sisters of the Child Jesus in Lepuy, France, to work with Bishop Paul Durieu at the Squamish mission in 1899.

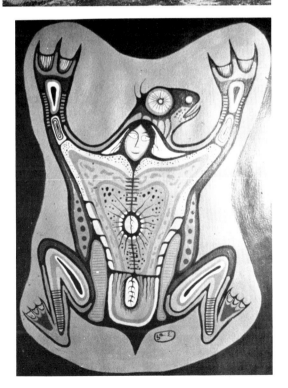

Plate 32. Painting in the Cree–Ojibway style by Saul Williams.

Plate 33. Norval Morrisseau and daughter Victoria with an early painting, "Sacred Bear" (1963).

Plate 34. "My Four Wives" (1976), by Norval Morrisseau.

was thus created when the federal government played realpolitik and stuck Wisconsin with a new territory it did not want. The state, which became, in effect, a "mother country," endeavored to make the country pay its own way and even yield a profit to the state, and encouraged exploitation of Menominee resources to serve the larger interests of non-Menominee residents of the state.

The termination plan, which provided for "indirect rule" in a show of native leadership and institutions, corporation and county, actually assured that real power would be exercised by outsiders representing Wisconsin's political, business and professional interests.[32]

As a result of the chaos which developed in the reservation communities which were terminated, the American government acknowledged its mistake and took steps to repeal its termination policy at the very time that the Canadian government was embarking on its 1969 termination strategy. Canadian government officials completely ignored the fifteen-year experience with the same policy in the United States. This blatant disregarding of facts, especially the serious consequences of such a policy for Indian people, can only be interpreted to mean that officials concerned are deliberately engendering cultural genocide. It is inconceivable that such policies are still pursued out of mere ignorance and ethnocentrism.

The elimination of reserve lands inevitably means the termination of status and rights for Indian people. The easiest way to destroy the distinctiveness of Indian people and their cultural heritage is to eliminate the land base. The forced change of status of Indian governments to that of municipal governments and the change of reserve land status from federal crown land to provincial crown land is a sure means of termination of Indian rights and status and elimination of a land base. Fundamental to the government's policy of termination of Indian status are municipal government status for tribal government and provincial jurisdiction over Indian matters. This was clearly spelled out in the 1969 White Paper, and as demonstrated above, they are the critical elements in local government guidelines for band councils and in the terms of reference for government programmes presently being implemented.

LAND CLAIMS

The crucial issues of reserve lands and Indian government status are also the key elements of the federal government's position on land claims. The James Bay Agreement of 1975 establishes the principle of provincial programme jurisdiction, provincial government ownership of mineral resources on reserve lands, and the incorporation of Indian band governments as municipal authorities.[33] The same kind of agreement is being proposed to the Indians of the Yukon.[34]

It is in the area of land claims that the discrimination against Indian people by the Canadian government is most blatant. In 1948, the Canadian government was prepared to accept Newfoundland into Confederation, despite the poverty of the people and presumably despite the lack of any aboriginal rights to Canadian status. Today, the people of Newfoundland enjoy not only their own provincial government but also a guaranteed share of the national revenue. In addition, they are granted special assistance because of their poverty.

Prince Edward Island is another example of the government's willingness to recognize the special needs of people without jeopardizing their right to self-government or removing jurisdiction over their own lands. In 1970, at the time the Canadian government was promoting its termination policy for Indians, it offered $50 million to more than 250,000 Indians through the Indian Economic Development Fund while at the same time it granted $725 million to Prince Edward Island, which has a population of less than half the number of Indians in Canada and a land base only a fraction of the size of the 2,209 reserves in Canada.[35]

Most recently, the federal government has refused to consider the Déné Declaration proposal to enter the Déné and their lands into Confederation through negotiations based on the principle of retention of aboriginal rights. The minister of Indian affairs and northern development has been given a mandate by the cabinet of the Canadian government to negotiate only the extinguishment of aboriginal rights and titles in the non-treaty areas. The rights granted to the people of Newfoundland and Prince Edward Island are denied the Déné of the Northwest Territories on the specious argument that their rights to have political jurisdiction over their lands and the right to their own government would be an acceptance of racism. This stance also contradicts the efforts of the federal government's policy in promoting respect and acceptance of the French people of Canada. The refusal of the Canadian government to recognize that the Déné have the right to their own languages and cultural practices and the institutional and economic means to sustain such rights is a denial of fundamental human rights. Paradoxically, the government supports these fundamental principles through its endorsement of the United Nations International Bill of Rights and its covenants on economic, social, and cultural rights and civil and political rights; as well as the United Nations Declaration on the Human Environment.

George Manuel explains the current position of native leaders in the following passage:

> It was the demand for home rule and responsible government in Upper and Lower Canada that gave rise to an enduring partnership among

the provinces of Canada and between the dominion and her mother country. When Quebec and Canada were united as one province for twenty-five years they discovered that responsible government without home rule is meaningless. Confederation guaranteed local autonomy, at least for the two major powers participating. The smaller and poorer Maritime provinces demanded grants that would provide them with the economic power to participate in Confederation and allow a financial base on which to enjoy their local autonomy. Prince Edward Island and Newfoundland stayed out of Confederation until they achieved terms they considered favourable. The New Brunswick government, which agreed to terms its people found unfavourable, was defeated and a more responsible and representative government took its place. If the western provinces and British Columbia appear to have accepted whatever they could get at the different times they entered Confederation, they have never stopped pressing their demands since they have been allowed to sit at the negotiating table.

The demand of Indian people that we be allowed to sit at the table where our lives are being negotiated, where our resources are being carved up like a pie, is not really very different from the demand made by every non-Indian group in Canada who share both a common history and a common territory. The whole history of Canada has largely been one long negotiation about the distribution of economic and political power.[36]

There are many more examples of the discrepancy between the treatment of Indian people and other groups of Canadians, and this discrepancy is being perpetuated through the terms of agreements respecting our aboriginal rights that the government is imposing across Canada. A comparison of the federal and provincial grants available to non-Indian local governments and the monies made available to band councils through the Department of Indian Affairs would demonstrate the paucity of the Indians' share of revenue to be used to provide essential services in housing, transportation, infrastructure, education, and health (to mention only a few).

The question of Indian self-government and status are critical issues in land claims negotiations and should not be dictated by government, particularly in view of long-term implications and consequences. To quote George Manuel:

No negotiation is possible that does not begin with an exercise of imagination that permits a good deal of give and take to reshape the present framework into something mutually acceptable. The first exercise of imagination—even if the spirit of good will now present in Parliament is transmitted to the government—will be to realize that any settlement must necessarily be a long-range process, and allow the retention of a strong land base on which we can develop a viable economy for Indian people. The Indian and Inuit peoples have learned from the Alaska settlement the dangers of entering into an agreement before there has been a sufficient involvement of the local communities directly affected, with research into both the historical background and current needs of the people, and the potential of their natural resources for their own economic development.[37]

CONCLUSION

Cultural pluralism in Canada will remain no more than theory as long as the government of Canada continues to pursue its policy of termination of Indian status and refuses to recognize the need for Indian homelands and governments which reflect the cultural heritage of the Indian people. Cultural pluralism is impossible where the institutions expressing one group's culture are imposed on another group, consequently destroying them and their culture. To quote George Manuel again:

Remaining Indian means that Indian people gain control of the economic and social development of our communities, within a framework of legal and constitutional guarantees for our land and our institutions. Without those guarantees, our people and our institutions remain in a defensive position, and our only weapon is passive resistance. With the constitutional and material support to carry on that development, there would be no dilemma. The racial myths that were created to justify the seizure of our land base will only be fully dispelled when we have received the legal recognition of our effective title to the lands that remain to us, and sufficient grants to compensate for what is lost that we can afford to develop what does remain. Only then will we be able to demonstrate that there is no conflict between wanting to live comfortably and wanting to develop within our own traditional framework.

 The desire for legal recognition of our aboriginal and treaty rights has taken on a religious perspective. But, as in most natural or traditional religions, the spiritual has not been separated from the material world.

Recognition of our aboriginal rights can and must be the mainspring of our future economic and social independence. It is as much in the long-term interest of the non-Indian peoples of North America as in our own interest that we be allowed our birthright, rather than that governments and churches perpetuate the Christian conspiracy that renders us the objects of charity while others enjoy the wealth of our land.[38]

The paternalistic and colonial nature of the administration of Indian affairs, with its resultant exploitation and deprivation of Indian people, will continue until the people and government of Canada recognize the inherent racism of its refusal to recognize Indian rights to self-determination and survival as a people. Until the people and government of Canada recognize that the issues involved for the Indian people are no different than those which led to the establishment of Israel, the present issue of a homeland for the Palestinians, or the long struggle of the Basques of Spain for their self-determination, injustices will continue to be a matter of course in a Canadian Indian policy historically rooted in the goals of assimilation and termination.

Notes

[1]The evolution of Canada's Indian policy from pre-Confederation British colonialism to the 1969 White Paper is the subject of a recent paper by John L. Tobias, "Protection, Civilization, Assimilation: An Outline of Canada's Indian Policy," *Western Canadian Journal of Anthropology* 6, no. 2 (1976): 13–30 (hereafter cited as "Canada's Indian Policy"). Another recent treatment is by law professor Douglas Sanders, "Government Indian Agencies in Canada," an unpublished manuscript in the author's possession.
[2]Ibid. See also L. F. S. Upton, "The Origins of Canadian Indian Policy," *Journal of Canadian Studies* 6, no. 4 (1973): 51–61.
[3]Canada, *Statutes of Canada*, "An Act Respecting Indians" 1975, p. 2; Diamond Jenness, "1943 Plan for Liquidating Canada's Indian Problem within 25 Years," April 1943. Presented to Joint Committee for the Senate and House of Commons on Indian Affairs, 1946; John Tobias, "Indian Reserves in Western Canada: Indian Homelands or Devices for Assimilation?" to be published by Museum of Man, Mercury Series, Ottawa (hereafter cited as "Indian Reserves in Western Canada"); and Tobias, "Canada's Indian Policy."
[4]David Laird, "Our Indian Treaties," *Historical and Scientific Society of Manitoba* (1905); R. N. Wilson, "Our Betrayed Wards," memorandum to the government, April 1921, *Western Canadian Journal of Anthropology* 4, no. 1 (1974): 21–31; Tobias, "Indian Reserves in Western Canada"; and L. F. S. Upton, "The Origins of Canadian Indian Policy."
[5]Canada, Department of Indian Affairs, Jean Chrétien, minister of Indian affairs and northern development, "Statement of the Government of Canada on Indian Policy, 1969." Presented to the twenty-eighth Parliament, June 1969, Ottawa (hereafter cited as White Paper 1969).
[6]Ibid., p. 6.
[7]Ibid.
[8]Ibid., p. 5.
[9]Tobias, "Canada's Indian Policy," p. 16.
[10]Ibid., p. 17.

[11]Ibid., p. 18. The 1876 Indian Act (section 86) states: "the Superintendent-General...shall authorize some competent person to report whether the applicant is an Indian who, from the degree of civilization [a term never defined explicitly] to which he or she has attained, and the character for integrity, morality, and sobriety which he or she bears" should be eligible for a location ticket.

[12]Ibid.

[13]Ibid., p. 22.

[14]Ibid.

[15]Tobias, "Indian Reserves in Western Canada."

[16]Sanders, "Government Indian Agencies in Canada."

[17]Tobias, "Canada's Indian Policy."

[18]White Paper 1969, p. 9.

[19]Ibid.

[20]Tobias, "Canada's Indian Policy," p. 25.

[21]Canada, Department of Indian Affairs, Jean Chrétien, minister of Indian affairs and northern development, to Right Honourable P. E. Trudeau, 30 April 1971.

[22]White Paper 1969, p. 10.

[23]Canada, Governor General in Council, "Appropriation Act No. 1, 1970; Indian Economic Development Regulations," *Canada Gazette*, Part II, Vol. 106, No. 14, 26 July 1972.

[24]Harold Cardinal, *The Unjust Society* (Edmonton: Hurtig, 1969); Indian Chiefs of Alberta, *Citizens Plus* (Indian Association of Alberta, 1970).

[25]White Paper 1969, p. 6.

[26]Ibid.

[27]Canada, "Housing on Indian Reserves and Designated Indian and Inuit Settlements," draft memorandum to cabinet by minister of Indian affairs and minister of urban affairs, 22 January 1975.

[28]Canada, "Recommendation and Summary," by G. E. Bell, conference co-ordinator, Regional Directors' Conference, Kingston, Ontario, 4–6 November 1974.

[29]Canada, Department of Indian Affairs, "Program Circular D-1, General Terms and Conditions of the Local Government Program," 14 February 1975; "Program Circular D-2, Policy Guidelines Related to District Councils," 5 February 1975; "Program Circular D-3, Policy Guidelines Related to Core Funding," 17 February 1975; "Program Circular D-4, Policy Guidelines Related to Program Funding," 27 March 1975; "Program Circular D-5, Policy Guidelines Related to Band Manager Program Administration Costs," 27 March 1975.

[30]"Our Way," special supplement to *The Saskatchewan Indian* (Prince Albert: Federation of Saskatchewan Indians, 1975).

[31]Gary Orfield, "A Study of the Termination Policy" (National Congress of American Indians, 1966).

[32]Nancy Oestreich Lurie, "Menominee Termination: From Reservation to Colony," *Human Organization* 31 (1972): 257.

[33]Canada, "James Bay Agreement," Quebec City, 1975.

[34]Canada, "Draft for Discussion: Agreement in Principle" (for Yukon Native People), December 1975; Yukon Territory, "Draft—Agreement in Principle, Proposal from the Office of the Commissioner," December 1975.

[35]George Manuel and Michael Posluns, *The Fourth World* (Toronto: Collier-Macmillan of Canada, 1974), p. 259.

[36]Ibid., pp. 217–18.

[37]Ibid., p. 229. [Editors' Note: Some of the concerns about the Alaska settlement are enunciated in the speech by Harold Cardinal, found at the end of this book.]

[38]Ibid., pp. 221–22.

9

Birth of a Cree-Ojibway Style of Contemporary Art

SELWYN DEWDNEY

The emergence of distinctive graphic and plastic expressions by artists of native ancestry has reached a ferment of activity over the past two decades that can only be described as a creative explosion. Paintings, drawings, prints, engravings, and sculpture in both traditional and innovative styles have attracted wide public interest and enjoyed lively sales. More significantly, these media are contributing to, as well as reflecting, the current revival of native tribal identities and are breaking down the stereotyped public image of the Indian, nourished for so long by western movies and school textbooks. West Coast art, for example, although still focused on totem poles, is now recognized as having been produced by people who got around in boats instead of on horses.

But there are mysteries here. How does one account for this extraordinary revival of creative energy among peoples whose traditional values were assumed to have been eroded by the invading society past the point of no return? Can the credit go to our educational institutions, to the loosening of restrictions on the use of alcohol by native persons, to the aggressive activities of the American Indian Movement, or to the dramas and documentaries that are broadcasting the dilemmas of northern Amerindians faced with massive threats to their environment from control dams and pipelines, or arsenic, mercury, and radioactive pollution? How could it happen so swiftly? Why has it happened in some regions of Canada and not in others?

The first stirrings of change in traditional Amerindian art can be traced back more than a century to the wanderings of European artists in the Plains region. Men like Catlin, Bodmer, Rindisbacher, and Kane brought with them painting techniques and approaches that were scanned with keen interest by the people they painted and particularly by shamans envious of their magical skills. Some asked for and got instruction, especially from Bodmer. At Fort Marion in Florida a number of Cheyenne, captured in the United States cavalry campaigns in the 1860's and 1870's, were given art materials and instruction that resulted in the remarkable collection of sketches and water colours recently reviewed and published by Karen Petersen.[1] As these men aged, however, and memories of the days of glory faded, little was heard of native painting until the late 1920's when a group of talented young Kiowa were enrolled as special students in the University of Oklahoma Art School. A few years later art classes for promising native students were opened at the Santa Fe Native Art School. A generation later the influence of these schools was evident in the work of a promising young artist of mixed Shoshone and Cree origin, Sarain Stump, whose career was tragically terminated by his death by drowning in Mexico.

Another artist, influenced by the romanticism and narrative trend of Plains art, was the Prairie Cree, Gerald Tailfeathers. Alex Janvier, a Chipewyan from northern Alberta, after proving his talent in an Alberta art school, was able to develop a powerful painting identity of his own in work that combined the brilliant colours of his people's craft work in designs that subtly suggested legendary themes. Encouraged by a Saskatoon art teacher, and promoted by a medical friend, another Prairie Cree, Allen Sapp, began to paint, although he showed no interest in traditional native styles. His visual reminiscences of his childhood on the reserve, in subdued greys and browns, are quite literal representationally, but they are so evocative and intimate that they could have been painted by no one who had not grown up in that milieu.

Meanwhile a young Ontario Ojibway, Arthur Shilling, from the Rama Reserve near Orillia, attended the Ontario College of Art and became a skillful portrait painter of his own people in the French Impressionist style, latterly developing his approach into expressionistic renderings that suggest a growing native identity.

And in the high Arctic, following the appointment of a non-native artist, James Houston, as community development officer, there emerged at Cape Dorset on Baffin Island an extraordinary and almost inexplicable outburst of sculpture. With Houston's encouragement and government support, the movement fanned out into Inuit communities throughout the central and eastern Arctic. A decade later, Houston brought back block printing techniques from Japan to initiate a wave of printmaking that is still peaking in a dozen far northern settlements. This is not to say that the Inuit had previously lacked plastic or graphic talents, for they were already skilled ivory carvers and engravers, but the scale and naturalism of the new sculpture and the graphic range of the printmaking media were without precedent. Northwest Coast artists, on the other hand, are producing art in many media —some of them acquired through conventional art training—but their style is unmistakably traditional, with roots that are recognizable far back into prehistory. The dominant eye–mouth motif, for example, can be found on coastal petroglyphs thousands of years old.

I do not propose here, and indeed I lack the background, to explore any further this continental florescence of native art. But, by sheer good luck, at a place and point in time when a single untaught artist was to initiate an extraordinary movement among young Cree and Ojibway, unique in style and content and still burgeoning today, I was there.

The year was 1960; the place Red Lake, a mining community one hundred miles north of Kenora and only fifty miles east of the Manitoba boundary. In the course of a systematic search for aboriginal rock paintings and petroglyphs, I had come here to follow up the report of rock paintings in the area. But I also brought with me a letter that I had received a month earlier, in June, from an Ontario Provincial Police constable, Robert Sheppard, who wrote, in part:

> Enclosed are some crayon drawings of a young Indian I have met from around Beardmore way. His crayon drawings are good and his water colours are even better. I have some of his water colours inside birch baskets and they are beautiful. His name is Norval Morrisseau.... Enclosed with the picture stories you will find the stories written out.... What do you think this boy's chances are? He can draw and paint, grew up with the people and knows the stories by heart. It seems a shame that his talents can't be made useful and available.

A week later, in a letter to my wife (13 July), I described my meeting with Morrisseau: "Sunday morning we took a L&F kicker over to Mackenzie Island, and spent most of the day with Bob.... interviewing the amazing Norval Morrisseau." And the following day:

> we broke camp, picked up our laundry, and drove over to Cochinour to view more paintings of Norval's that had been bought by a Dr. Weinstein [medical officer at the mine where Norval was beginning work]...he studied medicine—and painting—in Paris.... What to do about Norval filled most of the hour and a half I had with Weinstein. It was a really weird experience the day before meeting an Indian who (a) was filled with a deep pride of race, origin and identity (b) was almost a stereotype of everything you expect to find in an artist: sensitivity, a sureness about what he wanted to paint, didn't want to paint, liked and rejected, complete disinterest in money and material rewards.

Although Dr. Weinstein had supplied Morrisseau with art materials and bought his paintings, he wisely refrained from giving him any art instruction. But he had allowed him full access to an extensive library of art reproductions from three continents that he and his wife had collected over years of interest in the art of preliterate peoples. Despite a certain technical clumsiness these early paintings revealed a sureness of form and style, indeed an *authority*, that convinced me Morrisseau must have had access to a pictorial tradition of some sort. There simply had to be a source or sources. Perhaps he had found it in Weinstein's library. A day or two later Norval and I were invited to the Weinstein's for supper. I asked Norval to pick out the books of reproductions that had interested him most. Without hesitation he selected two: one of Navajo art, the other of West Coast painting and sculpture. Yet, scanning the contents of either to compare them with Morrisseau's work in the same room, it was clear to me that although there were a few instances where subjects coincided, the styles were poles apart. As the young Ojibway artist stated in my first interview: "My idea is, why I draw them—see, there's lots of stories that are told in Ojibway. But that wasn't enough for me. I wanted to draw them—*that's from my own self* [italics added]—what they would look like."

How was this possible? Could a single untaught native artist without exposure to any graphic or plastic tradition visualize and render such strong forms "out of his own self"? Surely Morrisseau had been influenced, however unconsciously, if not by his recent acquaintance with Weinstein's library then by some native source. Perhaps I should take a closer look at the rock paintings I had been recording. Or had he access to aboriginal pictography on hide or birchbark of which I had then only a peripheral acquaintance?

Over the years the questions continued to haunt me. In 1957, commissioned by the Royal Ontario Museum's ethnologist, Kenneth E. Kidd and funded by the Quetico Foundation, I had begun a field programme that was to extend over the following two decades from the Rockies to the Atlantic. This was a systematic search to find and record aboriginal rock art: forms painted over rock faces or abraded into their surfaces in many kinds of locations—rock walls in the foothills and deeper coulees, boulders on Prairie hilltops, shore rocks in the Canadian Shield woodlands and the Kejimkujik area of Nova Scotia. Rock paintings predominate in the Shield woodlands, totalling some three hundred sites scattered over an area of half a million square miles. The ethnological evidence that a majority of these were produced by shamans to record or reinforce the power of dreams induced by fasting is supported by the extreme individuality of the petroglyphs. Even in the region between Lake Winnipeg and Lake Superior, where the greatest concentration is found, stereotypes are so rare that the paintings cannot be said to have any distinctive style, which in itself rules them out as a source of Morrisseau's images. Nor do the Prairie petroglyphs suggest a credible source.

But Plains pictography on bison hide robes and tipi coverings offers a more likely source. Marius Barbeau[2] reproduced hide paintings collected in the eighteenth century for the French Dauphin's education. These are in a special diplay case in the Musée de l'Homme in Paris, and on a visit there in 1968 I was shown a dozen more in storage. All the later hide paintings feature raids, hunting events, or calendrical "winter counts," referring directly to actual experiences. Morrisseau, on the other hand, depicts supernatural beings, legendary events, or visionary experiences. Stylistically his work is poles apart from Prairie pictography, his large forms dominating the space whereas the figures on hide are small and numerous against broad vistas of empty background.

The pictographic practices that come closest to providing a source for Morrisseau's style have prevailed wherever the paper birch grew. Native leaders who signed the early treaties did so with their own marks: visual images on birchbark which signify their names and frequently their clan affiliations. Trail messages, once drawn pictographically on birchbark, have been superseded since the turn of the century by the syllabic system invented by a Methodist missionary a century ago, which has proven so successful that children today pick it up from their parents. Invariably Morrisseau signs his paintings in these syllabics, rendering the Ojibway words for "Copper Thunderbird," a name given him by a medicine woman when he was barely out of his teens.

There can be no doubt that birchbark pictography was in use long before European contact. Song records, usually less than a foot in length and only three or four inches wide, were inscribed with pictorial symbols by a shaman for a client to enable him to learn and remember a sequence of words and music literally dreamed up by the former to meet the client's problem, whether to attract a lover or destroy an enemy. Early in the eighteenth century, migrants out of Sault Ste. Marie, largely of Algonkian origin, but developing year-round village life due to the influence of Huron refugees and the generous food resources of the south shore of Lake Superior,[3] adapted birchbark pictography to teach and reinforce the message of an emerging healing ceremony known as the *Midéwewin*. An accumulating body of origin traditions and ceremonial procedures was passed on tutorially from master to initiate, aided by an increasingly sophisticated pictography which could be used mnemonically by the initiated. This religion spread out of centres in Minnesota into adjacent Canada, but it was modified more and more by local shamans as it penetrated farther into the hinterland. Morrisseau himself provides evidence[4] that this influence had reached the west shore of Lake Nipigon and that his grandfather had witnessed modified *Midé* rites in that area. However, these practices had died out in northern regions by 1930,[5] and Morrisseau was born too late—1934—to have had any exposure to *Midé* pictography. Yet, among people whose self-esteem had been reduced to the lowest point in their history, the young artist's pride in his Ojibway identity could only have been nourished by his grandfather's awareness of the status and achievements of the southern Ojibway cultivated by the *Midéwewin*.

In 1962, three years after Weinstein and Sheppard had discovered Morrisseau, he was re-discovered by Jack Pollock, a young artist from Toronto who was hoping to open his own commercial gallery in the fall. While visiting Thunder Bay he heard of Morrisseau's talent and tracked him down at the tiny shack town bordering Beardmore's town dump. Norval's work so impressed him that he arranged a one-man show in Toronto. This was a sell-out, and Morrisseau's paintings were a sensation. An on-again-off-again relationship with Pollock as his agent, along with an irregular flow of publicity in the media, kept the Ojibway artist's image alive and growing. With an exhibition in 1966 at the Musée du Québec and a large mural in the North American Indian Pavilion at Expo 67, Morrisseau began to be known internationally. Meanwhile, through visits to his wife's home in distant Big Sandy Lake, to Geraldton where his mother was living, and to other northwestern Ontario centres, he was becoming known to many aspiring young Cree and Ojibway who were fascinated by his success as well as by his renderings of oral traditions with which they, too, were familiar.

Even Daphne Odjig, a mature woman from Manitoulin Island who had emerged a decade earlier than Morrisseau and established herself as a professional artist in Winnipeg, reflected Morrisseau's influence in a limited way. But the real impact of his success was felt by the young Cree–Ojibway of northwestern Ontario and adjacent Manitoba, especially in the communities of Island Lake, Big Sandy Lake, and Red Lake. Carl Ray and Jaxon Beardy were early followers and more recently Saul Williams and Johnson Meekis. At Red Lake the Kakegamic brothers, Goyce and Josh, have set up a silk screen shop, reproducing their own work and that of others on fabrics and paper. Edward Cobiness hails from Buffalo Point in Manitoba, even farther west. Eastward an impressive number of "disciples" have made a place for themselves: Roy Thomas and Noel Ducharme in Thunder Bay; Francis Kakige, James Simon, and Blake Debassige from Manitoulin Island; Leo Yerxa of Couchiching; and Benjamin Chee Chee from Temagami, close to the Quebec border.

Like Morrisseau, all these artists—and others regretfully overlooked—are devoting their considerable talents to visual imagery based on oral traditions and ranging from representations of such powerful supernaturals as Wendigo or the Sacred Bear to personal fantasies and allegories. Variations on a motif that Morrisseau originally called a "medicine ball" appear so frequently as to have become almost a trade mark of the Cree-Ojibway school. Undulating "power lines" (a link with *Midé* pictography), hooked projections, and interior detail that is sometimes decorative and sometimes figurative are all features characteristic of Morrisseau's work. So is the frequency of composite forms, linked with or merging into or out of other forms—a style that has been developed with great ingenuity by Josh Kakegamic. One indication of a promising future is the fact that fully half of the Morrisseau school are still under thirty.

Perhaps the most important development has been the proliferation of silk-screen shops devoted to the reproduction of these paintings. Here the common feature of flat colour areas and clearly defined outlines lends itself perfectly to serigraph printing. A limited but brilliant palette also lends itself to low printing costs so that limited editions of signed prints can be marketed at prices the general public can afford. Indeed the whole movement promises to achieve as great a commercial success story as Inuit art.

In a recent radio interview I asked Norval what he thought of his young followers. He seems to be neither flattered nor impressed. Rather he voiced his fear that a majority were jumping on a commercial band wagon. He himself has a shrewd ability to survive the financial crises he not infrequently creates for himself. But money is not important to him. The day after his first show, he went down to Eaton's and spent—so the story goes—nearly a thousand dollars. This I could believe after visiting his home in Red Lake, where he showed me lengths of exotic silk materials and an enormous teapot that he had picked up in Toronto for his wife Harriet. But I have always taken seriously what he said to me at our first meeting, that he was painting "not for myself, for my people. Even if I don't get no money I would be glad to paint them just for my people to see."

But I have yet to attempt to explain how such a powerful influence on young Cree and Ojibway artists could emerge out of the bush country of northwestern Ontario. And I believe that the clue to the mystery—if there is any clue to the emergence of a major artist—has to lie in Norval's life as a boy on the trapline and his relationship with his grandfather, Moses Nanakonagos, with whom he lived during the most impressionable period of his childhood. Here I take refuge in what I wrote in my introduction to his *Legends of My People, the Great Ojibway*:

Emerging at sunrise from his cabin on Sand Point Reserve, the dark-eyed child searched the mists that wraithed the reaches of Lake Nipigon, yearning to sight one of the huge birds that might at that very moment be hunting horned snakes out there. Were there young thunderbirds now in the great stone nest at the summit of the hill above the cabin, the nest that no man had seen? Last night, lying on the rough cabin floor that was his bed, he had listened to the soft cadences of his native tongue as his grandfather told him how the mysterious Maymaygwessiwuk, with their strange hairy noseless faces, would emerge from their home in the living rock, paddling their stone canoe. In winter, as man and boy stopped on the trapline trail to boil a pail of tea, the lad would beg for another story about Wesuhkaychauk....So Moses would begin, gesturing and posturing with droll mimicry, until the mischievous shaman-hero of their people came alive, and the tea grew cold.

Dire predictions have been made about the future of native art. Already the critics are pointing to the disappearance of the Inuit hunting culture and the loss of an intimacy with the Arctic ethos as evidence of a declining identity while they ignore the escalating fantasies of Eskimo printmakers. Or they disparage revivals in the West of potlatch or sun dance ceremonies as watered down, "acculturated" versions of the "pure" originals. Rather, in my opinion these revivals are evidence of the growing strength of peoples whose deeper identities it has been impossible to suppress. I must confess that with respect to Morrisseau's art I, too, have been tarred with this brush. Yet time and again, although he has gone through plateaus and even declines in the quality of his art, he has re-emerged with new power and vigour, still the fountainhead of inspiration for young Cree and Ojibway who follow in increasing numbers the trail where his moccasins have left their deep imprints.

My most recent meeting with Norval Morrisseau was in February 1977 when we met with Jack Pollock in the latter's studio to tape two three-way interviews jointly arranged by the C.B.C. and the Ontario Educational Communications Authority.[6] The last time I had seen Norval had been more than three years before in Kenora, early on a Sunday morning when he had prevailed on me to lend him an amount which I knew was the local price of a bottle of bootleg booze. In Toronto I learned that he had lost the compulsion to drink more than a year ago, had even stopped smoking, and felt no urge for either. His alcoholism had, as he put it, "just dropped away." I had already seen the reproduction of a painting he had made since that happened, entitled "My Four Wives" which I assumed had a symbolic significance of some sort; but regardless of interpretation revealed a new surge of creativity. In our interview I learned that he had painted visionary visits to a former life in which he had been a powerful shaman and that he had experienced meeting these four women so vividly that he knew their names, ages, and personalities. Later I learned that he had made contact in Toronto with proponents of an ancient Tibetan value system known as Eckankar, and had acquired a firm belief in "soul-travel" and reincarnation. Always accessible to dreams and visionary episodes, he now makes long visits into the past. As he puts it, it is "the spiritual" that interests him. Yet already, though he verbally expresses ideas borrowed from the East, his unique powers of visual imagery have begun to incorporate them—as he did his grandfather's stories—into his highly individualistic paintings and to make them uniquely his own.

Morrisseau has changed; his paintings have changed. Of his followers, some will strike out for themselves, as several already have; others will change with him. But today the native peoples of Canada are too intimately in contact with the mainstream society to go back to "pure" traditions. Rather, as Wilfred Pelletier suggests,[7] a race with the flexibility and capacity for adaptation that has enabled its descendants to populate two continents and to survive the millenia since the ancestral migrations into the western hemisphere is as likely to incorporate those of other ancestries who live in North America into an Amerindian value system as we are to assimilate them. In reaffirming a proud native identity through their art, the aboriginal peoples of boreal North America may be instinctively preparing for a significant role in the present era of kaleidoscopic change with its totally unpredictable future.

Notes

[1]Karen Petersen, *Howling Wolf: A Cheyenne Warrior's Graphic Interpretation of His People* (Palo Alto, Ca.: American West, 1968), and *Plains Indian Art from Fort Marion* (Norman: University of Oklahoma Press, 1971).

[2]Marius Barbeau, *Indian Days on the Western Prairies*, Department of Northern Affairs and Natural Resources Bulletin no. 163, Anthropological Series no. 46 (Ottawa: National Museum of Canada, 1960).

[3]See my own *Sacred Scrolls of the Southern Ojibway* (Toronto: University of Toronto Press, 1975).

[4]In his *Legends of My People, the Great Ojibway* (Toronto, 1965).

[5]See Irving Hallowell, "Passing of the Midewewin in the Lake Winnipeg Region," *American Anthropology* 38 (1936): 32–51.

[6]O.E.C.A. reference nos. 511501 and 511502. The tapes were aired 8 February and 17 March 1978.

[7]In Wilfred Pelletier and Ted Poole, *No Foreign Land* (New York: Pantheon Books, 1973).

10

Philosophy and Psychology of Native Education

JOSEPH E. COUTURE

To provide a background for the philosophical and psychological observations to be made later, it will be useful to recount a number of salient events in the recent history of Indian education in Canada. Many native people have directly experienced the whole sequence of church schools, residential schools, day schools, government schools. Many were deeply affected by the 1959 forced integration policy based on an inane understanding of "equal opportunity for all," regardless of the nature of student need and regardless of the inadequacy of school programmes for non-native students as well as native.

Further to the 1959 policy, there were two other significant events. The presentation of *Citizens Plus*, better known as the *Red Paper*, to the federal government in 1970 was a singular historical moment.[1] That date was the first time in Canadian history that Indians developed and presented their own statement to Canada, including a statement on Indian education. The second outstanding moment occurred in the fall of 1972 on Vancouver Island, when for the first time native elders convened for two weeks to discuss with native leaders and workers the issues of the day. That conference was a trailblazer: it provided direction and inspiration to the participants. It changed peoples' lives.

What happened at that now famous seaside meeting? Twelve days of meetings were held, and for two of those days education was the central theme. At the end of the discussions, Louis Crier, on behalf of the elders present, rose to summarize the elders' thought, particularly with reference to the crucial questions of being and becoming an Indian, school systems, educational programmes, and Indian identity. He presented several broad survival principles which in substance were stated as follows:

> In order to survive in the twentieth century, we must really come to grips with the white man's culture and with white man ways. We must stop lamenting the past. The white man has many good things. Borrow.

Use his technology. Discover, define the harmonies between the two Cultures, between the basic values of the Indian Way and those of Western Civilization—and thereby forge a new and stronger sense of identity. To be fully Indian today, we must become bilingual and bicultural. We have never had to do this before. But, in so doing we will survive as Indians, true to our past. We have always survived. Our history tells us so!

That statement, in the scheme of native events, was a dramatic instant. Following Louis' presentation, the native workers and leaders present sat overwhelmed, awed. A pensive silence ensued. Finally, we asked the Old People: "How do you do that bicultural thing? How do you borrow that which is good and harmoniously integrate it?" The elders leaned back, smiled, and then said: "We've given you the general direction. You've got the education and training. You work it out!"

That moment symbolized a significant raising of consciousness in the native mind. The focus of this development in awareness bore out the central importance of native elders. It also marked the beginning of important changes and improvements in Indian education generally. It is a matter of record that, since the early 1970's, elders, usually under pressure from younger natives, are resuming their traditional role and prominence, a manifest role variously expressed as teacher, counselor, interpreter of history, expert on survival. *The* experts on native survival and history interpreted their people's history to their own people in terms of the contingencies of the day. A new optimism and a new vision grew out of that day. The elders pointed to a new direction for their people. With that mandate, a new energy, literally, began to spread across the land.

Since that time, many leaders in native education have been working out that "new direction." I would like to present my personal progress report through two broad sets of observations—one philosophical in nature and the second of a psychological order. I would very much like to give you some feel, some taste, for what Indians really do have to offer. I would strongly recommend Vine Deloria's *God is Red*[2] which clearly and provocatively underscores the relevance of the Native presence on this continent.

Relating to Indian tribes across the country in the initial stages can be a very confusing experience. The confusion arises from confrontation with a wide variety of languages and customs. However, if the effort is made to peel away what is peculiar to each tribe and region of the order of language and custom, one can begin to discern some common traits. These traits, when considered from both a philosophical and psychological viewpoint, can be perceived as authentic value-bridges between the two general cultures. I would like to emphasize that I do not consider natives as a superior race.

I am suggesting, however, that Indians do have something of a qualitative nature, and I wish to draw your attention to it.

Speaking as a working psychologist, and after many years in Indian country, as a child and as an adult, I am amazed by what I perceive to be the unusual human development of Indian man as embodied in the elders. In a sense, Indians have found a way of high human development. Education —from the Latin *educere*, which means to draw out, to develop human potential—in a traditional Indian context comprised means and ways which developed human potential to a degree greater than that generally observable in Western society. I heard a gentleman affirm recently in an eastern university: "Who really knows what lurks in the dark recesses of the Indian mind!" That statement is a classic in the category of superficiality.

First of all, when externals of language and custom are removed, one can observe virtually everywhere the characteristic qualities of what is referred to in Western philosophy as personalism. The essential thrust of an Indian philosophy of life, its dominant note, is that it is personalistic. Or again, holistic, humanistic, or existential—these terms can be used interchangeably.

Personalism means that Indian philosophy is person-centered. It does not focus on the person as object, but on the total person as something living, as a subject in a dynamic state of being–becoming. The traditional Western scholastic affirmation that "the subject and object of education is the whole of man in the whole of his environment for the whole of his life" applies completely to the Indian on this continent.

The development of a refined understanding of that fine Western tradition would significantly increase the effectiveness of non-Indians' attempts to relate to Indians. A simple but serious and consistent intellectual effort to understand and apply Western holistic theory would help develop the needed perceptions to authentic cross-cultural bridging and rapport. Western holism and personalism, it is contended, are essentially and substantially the same as native holism and personalism. Cognitive understanding would be a worthwhile beginning. However, let it be understood that for complete bridging, affective development, which is the more difficult of the two, is also essential.

A second philosophical comment points to the reality of what I would call "cosmic relationships." The most obvious example of this relationship is the so-called "closeness" of natives to nature. To envisage an Indian lying on a river bank under a shady tree in the middle of summer endlessly gazing out at nature is not to understand how natives are "close" to nature. The relationship is profound and not one consisting of romantic, mindless contemplation. The relationship is cosmic. When an Indian says that one has to learn the laws of nature, he is making a clear statement. That understanding is not the equivalent to the "natural law" concept of Western scholasticism. Suffice it to affirm that a native understanding of natural laws is of a cosmic and existential order, that life was lived according to such understandings, and that such living made for an intimacy with nature.

A final observation concerns the Indian relationship to the land. In *God is Red*, Deloria affirms that there is a qualitative difference between the two general cultures in their respective attitudes towards the land. In Western society land is prized as an object, something to be obtained, possessed, developed, or manipulated on the market, in order to make a profit; in traditional native society land is something alive which you relate to, as subject to subject. Therefore respect and a sense of stewardship are imperative. The title "Mother Earth" is something more than a childish expression. There is therefore a qualitative difference, an essential difference.

In addition to examining the teachings and statements of elders and the content of tradition, it is also worthwhile to analyse observable native behaviour, notably that of elders, who are not only models of what native education can produce, but also outstanding expressions of human development. They are superb embodiments of what being human can be all about.

These examples of unusual self-actualization, of development of the human potential, are of considerable consequence for native educational programmes. By observing the elders carefully, and by attempting to understand the what and why of their behaviour, we may learn the kind of person native education could be developing. The remarkable intelligence and wisdom, the excellent memory capacity and discursive ability—these are cognitive behaviours which students would do well to examine in order to discover what psycho-cultural variables combine to induce such high-level development of the faculties. Then, there is the affective dimension of elders' behaviour: for instance, their sense of humour, of caring, of finesse in teaching and counselling.

Please don't take offense if I say to those of you who have gone through a Western educational system—and I am one of you—that we are "half-brained." What do I mean by that? Recent research, notably that of Robert Ornstein and his followers, such as Semples and Wilson, strongly suggests that there is physio-psychological evidence pointing to a distinction between left brain activity and right cerebral function and that our school systems, including our best universities, have done little else but develop the left brain, the seat of intellectual analysis, linear thinking, and language. The development of the right side of the cerebrum—the seat of metaphorical and symbolic perception, the area of intuition—has been neglected. Our left brains are usually well developed, but our right brains are untended; therefore we are incomplete.

Traditional Indian educational processes addressed themselves to *both* sides of the brain, not consciously, but they did so nonetheless. A functioning native mind involved both hemispheric functions, not one to the forced exclusion of the other. A linear analytical mind cannot understand or appreciate the behaviour of a person who frequently moves in terms of his intuition. The analytical mind must break things down into controllable little pieces before it can comprehend. Such a mind experiences considerable difficulty in developing a relationship with one which is largely intuitive, actively metamorphic, and symbolic in expression. That is why one learned person did say, as referred to above, "Who knows what lurks in the dark recesses of the native mind." That is why, in everyday language, Westerners frequently observe, "Who can understand an Indian?"

Those who are investigating these various behaviours of the brain are making the claim that the next major revolution in education will be in terms of right brain development. This simply means finally addressing ourselves operationally, effectively, to the development of the total person and not just to a segment of the person. Teachers will soon learn how to develop affective and cognitive ability, intuitive and metamorphic ability and analytical thinking. That will then resemble Indian education.[3]

A second behavioural area awaiting the attention of such professionals as teachers, counselors, social workers, and others is that of native child-rearing practices. It is my observation that these practices foster free individuals and develop children who take full responsibility for what they do and what they become. This learning occurs because parents give their children the emotional and physical room to make mistakes, to fail, and to succeed. Such practices are person-centered.

Traditional decision-making is a third behaviour awaiting close examination. Virtually every tribe employed a consensus decision-making process, as opposed to decision-making based on a majority vote. We know that at times majority rule can by tyrannical, that a majority favouring something is not necessarily evidence that it is a humanizing decision. Traditionally, Indians did not make a group decision until everyone present indicated his feelings and thoughts. Time was taken for everyone to express himself and for everyone to move with confidence into a group decision. Such a process rides on the bedrock value of the importance of the individual as a responsible person. It was because of this process that native groups were able to resolve that standing paradox of how an individual might best become his unique self, while at the same time being responsible and intensely involved in communal interactions and mutual support systems. This process works only to the extent that the underpinning value remains that of the worth and uniqueness of the individual person.

The preceding discussion is a brief sketch of some fundamental native values and behaviours which, if closely examined, can form the basis for a native twentiety-century philosophy and psychology of education. It is strongly felt that the suggestions made have strong and clear implications for the teachers and administrators of native education at all levels. It is now possible to provide training for such people whereby both their own development as human beings is significantly tended to, and their skills to facilitate a humanizing educational process for others are notably developed.

Native education was once a development process that addressed the total person. It is now moving in that direction again. In the traditions of native education there are clear philosophical or psychological principles and a history to justify and promote that encouraging movement.

Notes

[Editors' note: see Marie Marule's paper for a fuller discussion of the implications of the 1969 Red Paper.]

[2](New York: Dell, 1973).

[3]Teachers, administrators, psychologists, and philosophers will find much in the series of some dozen books entitled *Studies of the Person*, edited by Carl Rogers (Columbus, Ohio: C. Merrill, 1969-) concerning the development of the whole man. See also R. Ornstein, *The Psychology of Consciousness* (San Francisco: Freeman, 1972); Bob Samples, "Learning with the Whole Brain," *Human Behaviour* (February, 1974): 17-23; and S. Wilson, "The Feeling Side of Teaching," Paper presented to the Cogito Conference, Toronto, 23 October 1975.

11

Treaties Six and Seven:
The Next Century*

HAROLD CARDINAL

I expect that many of you have heard, in various amounts of truth, different views and perspectives on the question of Indian people, their treaties, and their relationship to the general society. You have asked me to speak on Treaties Six and Seven, with a view to the next century. I am humbled by the request to speak on the topic of such fundamental importance to our people.

For us who are Indian, our treaties are both sacred and important. Not because they provide five dollars a year to us as individuals, or a walking plow and an ox to our bands, or a suit of clothes and brass buttons for our chiefs and councillors, or because of a medal, a flag, and a bow promised to our leaders.

Our treaties are sacred because they reaffirm our people's allegiance to their covenant with their Creator. The laws which govern that relationship are the trail upon which that relationship was to travel.

Our treaties are important because they mark a milestone in our history—a point in time at which we shared custodial responsibility for our lands in keeping with the agreement made by the founding father of our nation, an agreement witnessed and sanctioned by our Creator. The importance of understanding the concept of Indian treaties lies in two different areas, areas that have never been clearly understood by many people in this country before.

We are a nation of people, a people who were put on this continent with the specific purpose of fulfilling our responsibilities to our Creator, of fulfilling our responsibilities to our land. Ours was a special relationship with

*This paper is an edited transcript of the speech given at the concluding banquet held at the Calgary Convention Centre, 19 February 1978. The original tape and transcript were made by Val Jones of Kamloops, B.C., a delegate at the conference.

our Creator. A relationship that is analogous in many ways to that of the Jewish people. We too are a chosen people.

In many respects our elders perceived the treaties as a process whereby the white society, with its legal systems, with its systems of law, would guarantee to our people the right to continue practising their beliefs, the right to continue fulfilling their responsibilities to their Creator as was agreed upon since time began. Our elders intended that the treaties would tell the guests who came to our country that while we welcomed them to our country, and while we wanted to build a nation in partnership with other nations so that our children could grow up in a better environment, we also by the process of our treaties wanted to let other people know that our first allegiance, our first commitment, was not to a temporal power, but to our Creator.

When we Indians talk of treaties, whether we talk of those of one hundred years ago or of settlements in the 1960's, in the 1970's, or into the future, the act of making a treaty, the act of formally defining a relationship with others, means that a very basic choice is being made by us as collective units or as individuals. We are saying to all others, and to all things that are living, that we want to continue to pay our first homage, to pay our first allegiance to our Creator. We want to live by the laws that were set for us through many centuries, to fulfill those laws by the many varied and rich ceremonies that we have, and to be able to live within those laws on the basis of the morals and the values that we get from them so that we can treat each other as brothers and sisters, and so that we can treat our guests as brothers and sisters in this country. This is what we want to reaffirm, when we talk about our treaties, both in the past, the present, and in the future.

I think it is important that people begin to understand that when Indians talk about treaty and land claim settlements, we are talking about much more than just dollars for Indian development. We are talking about preserving the soul, the integrity of our Indian souls, the integrity of our Indian nations. That for us has been historically, is now, and will continue to be the primary consideration in talking about treaties.

There is a second level of consideration and that is the sharing, the accommodation, that took place between our people and the larger society. The question that we have to resolve, the question that has remained unresolved for the better part of one hundred years, is how best to guarantee an equitable distribution of wealth and resources to Indian people, and not only to Indian people, but to all Canadians, so that all people who live on this land can feel, can experience, the wealth and richness that this land has to offer.

In this respect, part of what happened in James Bay in the agreement with Quebec, part of what will happen in the Northwest Territories, part of what will happen in the Yukon and British Columbia and in all areas where no treaties have been signed is a process that will, it is to be hoped, result in an arrangement by which Indian people in this country can begin to overcome the problems of poverty that are far too evident in far too many of our communities.

I have had the opportunity in the past nine years to visit many Indian and non-Indian communities in this country and in many parts of the United States, to see how other peoples are handling their poverty problems. Most recently I had the fortune of visiting the native people in Alaska, to find out what has happened to those people since the signing of their billion-dollar settlement five years ago. The meetings we had with native people in Alaska were extremely useful and in many respects opened our eyes to many things that perhaps we were not aware of before.

The one point that hit us in an extremely strong way was the fact that even though the natives of Alaska received a billion dollars in settlement, this money was broken into a number of corporations, each of which was required to be a profit-making corporation. Because they were required by law to make a profit, those bodies were unable, in fact, to begin dealing with the very real social and economic problems faced by the native people in Alaska. And so, while you have a billion dollars available to corporate leaders, that money is not available to poor people, and naturally there is a growing tension between the leadership of the Alaskan natives and the shareholders of those companies.

But one point that was even more intriguing, as we in Canada begin looking at the process of resolving Indian claims, is the fact that the resolution of Indian claims is not going to be an easy process for Indian people. Even after the settlement was arrived at in Alaska, even after the billion dollars was committed by the federal government for settlement with the Alaska natives, and even after comprehensive laws were set up by both levels of government to implement that agreement extensively, we find five years later that the major effort of Alaska natives is being spent in trying to make sure that their billion-dollar agreement is being implemented.

It is a situation in which corporations, both individually and collectively through the Alaska Federation of Natives, have had to spend enormous amounts of energy, and enormous amounts of time, trying to ensure that all of the clauses were implemented in the manner understood by the Alaska natives. What has happened in the last five years is that the Alaska natives have been forced to fight, almost clause by clause, the agreement that they reached with the American government five years ago. It has reached the point where a lot of those clauses are still in court for interpretation by various committees of Congress or various other bodies set up by the American government.

We met with one corporation which received $11 million, ostensibly to develop business for its shareholders. Since the receipt of that $11 million, approximately $6 million has been spent on efforts, in lobbying activities, to make sure that the American Congress and the state legislatures implemented the agreement as was understood: in expenditures on legal fees, taking the American government and various other government agencies to court on interpretations of specific clauses with respect to the agreement; in court fees; and in consultant fees. Of the eleven million, only five million to date has been available for real economic development.

What does this mean in this country? We are now finding out through our brothers of the James Bay area who have had to come to our Parliament, who have had to bring their own lobbying effort to make sure that their agreement is implemented and followed as they understood that agreement to be, that it means that in this country Indian people are going to have to make a choice and are going to have to make a conscious decision about how their claims are going to be resolved.

It would be naive in the extreme for Indian people to assume that just because they have a written agreement with the government that their problems are over as soon as that agreement is signed. A lot of energy is going to have to be expended, and what Indian people have to choose is at what point in time they are going to expend their energies. Is it prior to the signing of an agreement or after the signing of an agreement? What kind of monetary, fiscal resources are going to be needed by native people, whether in this province or anywhere else in the country, to ensure that Indian claims in question of the implementation of Indian treaties are solved equitably? What kind of resources are they going to require, and how much involvement must all people have in the negotiation of these settlements?

One thing that is clear from the Alaskan experience that will be no different in this country is that wherever agreements are left rather vague, or wherever agreements are left up to bureaucrats to interpret and to implement, the responsibility of those government agencies, irrespective of who serves in those agencies, will be to try to give the narrowest possible interpretation, the narrowest possible technical base, and give as little as is possible to Indian people under the settlement.

And I think our people both in this province and throughout the country have to begin looking realistically at the type of political organizations they are going to require. They are going to have to try, perhaps for the first time, to put aside their petty differences and petty jealousies, to bring their efforts together, to try and pull the best minds together, both Indian and non-Indian, to ensure that in a few years time, perhaps we can begin seriously to solve the hard-core economic and social problems that our people face in this country. Unless we are able to resolve these problems, it is useless for us to look to a next century as a people, because we will never reach the next century as a people unless we overcome these problems.

Unless we are able to put aside our petty personal differences, and begin looking at our collective responsibilities to our children, my children, all of the children that are in this land, we are going to leave for those children an even more bitter legacy than the one we found upon coming into this society.

I think it must be clear, that there have to be limits on how much we trust people. There have to be limits on how much we trust government. And there have to be limits to how much we as a people trust the larger society. There has to be some trust, but that trust cannot be naive, because all we have to do is look at the conditions on our reserves to find out where naive trust has brought us.

We have to be hard in our assessment, we have to be realistic, and we have to be objective in our assessment of what we need to do. Above all, we have to be honest with one another as Indian people if we are going to be able to overcome the problems that we face.

We live in difficult times in this country. We have to be able to go back to our elders, from all tribes, from one end of the country to the other, to learn from those elders what the meaning of our nationhood is as a people. Because, as we begin to discover the meaning of that nationhood, maybe we can be of help to our white brothers, who are, in the next few years, going to be facing some pretty difficult questions amongst themselves regarding the future of Confederation.

Our commitment to our future, our commitment to our children, does not mean that we have no responsibilities to others who live on this land. Our interest as Indian people is perhaps equal to that of any government, any government official, or any citizen in terms of making sure that this country stays together. Our treaties were with the Crown that represented the whole country—not one-third of the country, not one-half of the country, but all of the country. Canada is *our land*; it is no one else's land; and it is in our interest as Indian people to make sure that that land stays together, for it is our children that are going to have to suffer the consequences if that does not take place.

For us to be able to do that, for us to be able to participate meaningfully in the coming discussions regarding the survival of this country, the only real basis and the only real resource we have as Indian people is to be able to go back to our elders, for them to explain to us what the meaning of our existence is and what the meaning of our country is, so that we can have something to share with our white brothers.

It is not adequate at this time, especially when there are such deep questions of division amongst the white people, it is not adequate for us to say that we have been screwed, that we have been hard done by, because no people in this country, no people in this world have a monopoly on injustice. At some point in history, at some point in time, all peoples have gone through some pretty rough times.

Our responsibility, the responsibility of our generation, is to be able to try to forget that those problems are there. Instead our energies must be channelled into trying to find solutions, so that we can offer those solutions, not only for our children but for other people as well.

I have talked about these matters because you asked me to talk about treaties in the next century. For those of you who are Indian, for those of you who are involved in various religious ceremonies that are Indian, you will find that the main responsibility of Indian people is to try to pass on their knowledge, to try to make sure that the elders pass on knowledge from one generation to the next to ensure that our people can continue to survive, so that our people can continue to live within the laws that were set for our people. But once in a while, many white people think that our history began when they arrived. Our history began with our Creation, and the vision of our elders begins at that point.

Those are the two points of our trail, as Indian people. In the process of developing a world outlook, a viewpoint within those two points, our people have evolved through many, many centuries certain values, certain thought processes. It is, for example, said by our elders that Indian people have a responsibility every one hundred years to reaffirm, not only the work that has been done by the generations of the preceding one hundred years, but to set the ground work for the succeeding one hundred years, and into the future as well, to make sure that the Indian trail goes beyond the past, goes beyond the present, and into the future.

For us who are Indian, and who happen to live in this part of the country, upon our generation has fallen the responsibility of ensuring that for the next one hundred years our people can continue to follow their trail. Upon our generation falls the responsibility of beginning to understand, and defining for the first time, the relationship that we should have as a people amongst each other, and, equally important, the relationship that we should have with those others who have come to our land.

What is our generation's responsibility? Commemorating the centennial of the treaties in this province or any part of this country means more than just having a pow wow to entertain our friends or our guests. It is an occasion far more important than one to be spent remembering the hurts, the aches, and the anxieties that we have had in the past. That occasion gives to us, as Indian people, a responsibility to make sure that the trail which began with our Creation and has travelled through many centuries will continue to travel for many more centuries into the future.

That is the point that our people must understand, and it is appropriate that others in Canada are having discussions about who they are and where they are going as a people, because we also by circumstance and by time are forced to go through that process. Unless we can understand that, and unless we can meet that responsibility with the strength that is inherent in our pipes and in our prayers, then our children will not have that much of a trail to follow in the future.

That is the responsibility that we have to look at as Indian people. For too long we have looked at each other as people from different tribes, who speak different languages, who do their dances perhaps a bit differently, who dress differently and do things in a different way. But whether we live in the pueblos in the southwest, the igloos of the north, the longhouse in the east, or the big house in the West, we are all members of the Indian nation. We are all members of a nation which has a special covenant with its Creator. We are all members of a nation which has its laws, no matter what the linguistic differences are amongst the different tribes. We are one people and our responsibility is the same no matter where we go in the North American continent. That has to be the lesson that our generation learns and that has to be the lesson that we pick from our brothers who are in the process of commemorating their centennial of Treaty Seven in 1977.

I have perhaps dwelt a bit too much on some aspects with regard to the question of Indian treaties, and the spiritual significance of those treaties, because that type of information is one that you will not find in law books or in academic records anywhere in the country. It is knowledge that our elders have and it is to them that we have to turn if we are going to be able to build any basis for the future. But recognizing who we are, as a people, and what we do as a people, has to be tempered by the type of hard-nosed business approach that we have to take when it comes to resolving the problems of poverty that our people face.

We as a people will never be given one inch, one concession, for nothing from the larger society. We are going to have to fight; we are going to have to create a dialogue; we are going to have to create the understanding. We are going to have to show the support that is required because every concession that we get, we are going to have to work to get and to ensure that it is implemented. If there was one mistake that was made in the past, and hindsight in any situation always gives 20–20 vision to people, but if there is one mistake that was made in the past it was that we trusted too much. It was our expectations that, having reached an agreement at one point, everything would fall into place.

One hundred years later we find, and I hope we have learned, that we must continue to be vigilant, we must continue to work on a daily basis both as individuals and collectively as Indian people, and collectively as people of this land to ensure that agreements are honoured and to ensure that all Canadians, or that all people who live on this land, benefit from and receive the blessings that our country has to offer.

A Selected Bibliography
on the Native Peoples of
Western Canada Since the "Making" of the Treaties

General

Cumming, P. A., and N. H. Mickenberg, eds. *Native Rights in Canada.* 2nd ed. Toronto: The Indian–Eskimo Association of Canada, 1972.

Graham–Cumming, G. "The Health of the Original Canadians, 1867–1967." *Medical Services Journal, Canada* (February 1967): 115–66.

Hawthorne, H. B., ed. *A Survey of the Contemporary Indians of Canada: Economic, Political, Educational Needs and Policies.* 2 vols. Ottawa: Indian Affairs Branch, 1966–67.

Jamieson, Kathleen. *Indian Women and the Law in Canada: Citizens Minus.* Ottawa: Minister of Supply and Services Canada, 1978.

Jenness, Diamond. *The Indians of Canada.* 1932. Reprint. Toronto: University of Toronto Press, 1977.

Loram, C. T., and T. F. McIlwraith, eds. *The North American Indian Today: University of Toronto–Yale University Seminar Conference, Toronto, September 4–16, 1939.* Toronto: University of Toronto Press, 1943.

Patterson, E. P. *The Canadian Indian: a History since 1500.* Don Mills, Ont.: Collier–Macmillan, 1972.

Price, John A. *Native Studies. American and Canadian Indians.* Toronto: McGraw-Hill/Ryerson, 1978.

Raby, Stewart. "Indian Land Surrenders in Southern Saskatchewan." *Canadian Geographer* 17 (1973): 36–52.

Tobias, J. L. "Indian Reserves in Western Canada: Indian Homelands or Devices for Assimilation." In *Approaches to Native History in Canada: Papers of a Conference held at the National Museum of Man, October, 1975,* edited by D. A. Muise, pp. 89–103. Ottawa: National Museums of Canada, 1977.

———. "Protection, Civilization, Assimilation: An Outline History of Canada's Indian Policy." *Western Canadian Journal of Anthropology* 6, no. 2 (1976):13–30.

The Nineteenth Century

Barbeau, Marius. *Indian Days on the Western Prairies.* Ottawa: Information Canada, 1965.
Dempsey, Hugh A. *Crowfoot. Chief of the Blackfeet.* Edmonton: Hurtig, 1972.
————. *Charcoal's World.* Saskatoon: Prairie Books, 1978.
Gresko, Jacqueline. "White 'Rites' and Indian 'Rites': Indian Education and Native Responses in the West, 1870–1910." In *Western Canada: Past and Present*, edited by A. W. Rasporich, pp. 163–82. Calgary: McClelland and Stewart West, 1975.
Hughes, Stuart. *The Frog Lake "Massacre": Personal Perspectives on Ethnic Conflict.* Toronto: McClelland and Stewart, 1976.
Jennings, John. "The Plains Indian and the Law." In *Men in Scarlet*, edited by Hugh A. Dempsey, pp. 50–65. Calgary: McClelland and Stewart West, 1974.
————. "Policemen and Poachers—Indian Relations on the Ranching Frontier." In *Frontier Calgary*, edited by A. W. Rasporich and Henry Klassen, pp. 87–99. Calgary: McClelland and Stewart West, 1975.
Morris, Alexander. *The Treaties of Canada with the Indians.* Toronto: Belfords, Clarke and Co., 1880; facsimile edition, Toronto: Coles, 1971.
Ray, Arthur J. *Indians in the Fur Trade: Their Role as Hunters, Trappers, and Middlemen in the Lands Southwest of Hudson Bay, 1660–1870.* Toronto: University of Toronto Press, 1974.
Sharp, Paul F. *Whoop-Up Country: The Canadian–American West, 1865–1885.* 1955. Reprint. Norman: University of Oklahoma Press, 1973.
Sissons, C. K. *John Kerr.* Toronto: Oxford University Press, 1946.
Stanley, G. F. G. *The Birth of Western Canada: A History of the Riel Rebellions.* 1936. Reprint. Toronto: University of Toronto Press, 1961.
Taylor, John L. "Canada's North-West Indian Policy in the 1870's. Traditional Premises and Necessary Innovations." In *Approaches to Native History in Canada: Papers of a Conference held at the National Museum of Man, October, 1975*, edited by D. A. Muise, pp. 104–10. Ottawa, National Museums of Canada, 1977.
————. "The Development of an Indian Policy for the Canadian North-West, 1869–79." Ph.D. dissertation, Queen's University, 1975.

The Twentieth Century

Adams, Howard. *Prison of Grass: Canada from the Native Point of View.* Toronto: New Press, 1975.

Brody, Hugh. *Indians on Skid Row: The Role of Alcohol and Community in the Adaptive Process of Indian Urban Migrants.* Ottawa: Department of Indian Affairs and Northern Development, Northern Science Research Group, 1971.

Burke, James. *Paper Tomahawks: From Red Tape to Red Power.* Winnipeg: Queenston House, 1976.

Campbell, Maria. *Halfbreed.* Toronto: McClelland and Stewart, 1973.

Cardinal, Harold. *The Unjust Society.* Edmonton: Hurtig, 1969.

———. *The Rebirth of Canada's Indians.* Edmonton: Hurtig, 1977.

Dosman, Edgar J. *Indians: The Urban Dilemma.* Toronto: McClelland and Stewart, 1972.

Frideres, J. S. *Canada's Indians. Contemporary Conflicts.* Scarborough, Ont.: Prentice-Hall, 1974.

Goodwill, Jean, ed. *Speaking Together. Canada's Native Women.* Ottawa: Secretary of State, 1975.

Jenness, Diamond. "Canada's Indians Yesterday: What of Today?" *Canadian Journal of Economics and Political Science* 20 (1954): 95–100.

LaRoque, Emma. *Defeathering the Indian.* Agincourt, Ont.: Book Society of Canada, 1975.

Manuel, George, and Michael Posluns. *Fourth World: An Indian Reality.* Don Mills, Ont.: Collier-Macmillan, 1974.

Price, Richard T. "Indian Land Claims in Alberta: Politics and Policy-Making (1968–77)." M.A. thesis, University of Alberta, 1977.

Robertson, Heather. *Reservations Are for Indians.* Toronto: James Lewis and Samuel, 1970.

Ryan, Joan. *Wall of Words: Betrayal of Urban Indians.* Toronto: Peter Martin Associates, 1978.

Wuttunee, William I. C. *Ruffled Feathers: Indians in Canadian Society.* Calgary: Bell Books, 1971.

The Plains Tribes

Ahenakew, Edward. *Voices of the Plains Cree.* Toronto: McClelland and Stewart, 1973.

Dempsey, Hugh A. *Indian Tribes of Alberta.* Calgary: Glenbow-Alberta Institute, 1978.

Ewers, John C. *The Blackfeet: Raiders on the Northwestern Plains.* Norman: University of Oklahoma Press, 1958.

Goldfrank, Esther S. "Changing Configurations in the Social Organization of a Blackfoot Tribe during the Reserve Period (the Blood of Alberta, Canada)." American Ethnological Society Monograph Series, no. 8 (1945).

Grinnell, George Bird. *Blackfoot Lodge Tales: The Story of a Prairie People.* 1892. Reprint. Lincoln: University of Nebraska Press, 1962.

Hanks, L. M. and J. R. Hanks. *Tribe under Trust: A Study of the Blackfoot Reserve in Alberta.* Toronto: University of Toronto Pres, 1950.

Hungry Wolf, Adolf. *The Blood People: A Division of the Blackfoot Confederacy. An Illustrated Interpretation of the Old Ways.* New York: Harper and Row, 1977.

Jenness, Diamond. *The Sarcee Indians of Alberta.* Ottawa: National Museum of Canada, 1938.

Kehoe, Alice B. "The Dakotas in Saskatchewan." In *The Modern Sioux: Social Systems and Reservation Culture,* edited by Ethel Nurge, pp. 148–72. Lincoln: University of Nebraska Press, 1970.

Kennedy, Dan. *Recollections of an Assiniboine Chief.* Edited by James R. Stevens. Toronto: McClelland and Stewart, 1972.

Laviolette, Gontran. *The Sioux Indians in Canada.* Regina: Marian Press, 1944.

Lewis, Oscar. "The Effects of White Contact upon Blackfoot Culture." American Ethnological Society Monograph Series, no. 6 (1942).

McClintock, Walter. *The Old North Trail; or Life, Legends and Religion of the Blackfeet Indians.* 1910. Reprint. Lincoln: University of Nebraska Press, 1968.

MacEwan, Grant. *Tatanga Mani: Walking Buffalo of the Stonies.* Edmonton: Hurtig, 1969.

Mandelbaum, David G. "The Plains Cree." *Anthropological Papers of the American Museum of Natural History* 37, no. 2 (1940): 155–316.

Schultz, J. W. *Blackfeet and Buffalo: Memories of Life among the Indians.* Norman: University of Oklahoma Press, 1962.

Snow, Chief John. *These Mountains are our Sacred Places: The Story of the Stoney People.* Toronto: Samuel Stevens, 1977.

The Métis

Bowsfield, Hartwell. *Louis Riel. The Rebel and the Hero.* Toronto: Oxford University Press, 1971.

Chalmers, John W. "Schools for Our Other Indians: Education of Western Canadian Metis Children." In *The Canadian West,* edited by Henry Klassen, pp. 93–109. Calgary: Comprint, 1977.

Flanagan, Thomas. "Catastrophe and the Millennium: A New View of Louis Riel." In *Religion and Society in the Prairie West,* edited by Richard Allen, pp. 35–52. Regina: Canadian Plains Research Center, 1974.

———. "Louis 'David' Riel: Prophet, Priest, King, Infallible Pontiff." *Journal of Canadian Studies* 9 (1974): 15–26.

————. "The Mission of Louis Riel," *Alberta History* 23 (1975): 1–12.

Giraud, Marcel. *Le Métis canadien: Son rôle dans l'histoire des provinces de l'ouest.* Paris: Institut d'Ethnologie, 1945.

Howard, Joseph Kinsey. *Strange Empire: A Narrative of the Northwest.* New York: William Morrow, 1952.

Lussier, Antoine S., and D. Bruce Sealey, eds. *The Other Natives: The Métis. Volume One, 1700–1885.* Winnipeg: Manitoba Métis Federation Press, 1978.

Sealey, D. Bruce, and Antoine S. Lussier. *The Métis. Canada's Forgotten People.* Winnipeg: Manitoba Métis Federation Press, 1975.

Stanley, G. F. G. *Louis Riel.* Toronto: Ryerson, 1963.

de Trémaudan, Auguste-Henri. *Histoire de la nation métisse dans l'ouest canadien.* Montreal: Editions Albert Levesque, 1935.

Woodcock, George. *Gabriel Dumont.* Edmonton: Hurtig, 1975.

The Pacific Coast

Drucker, Philip. *Cultures of the North Pacific Coast.* Scranton, Pa.: Chandler, 1965.

Duff, Wilson. *The Indian History of British Columbia. Volume 1. The Impact of the White Man.* Victoria: Provincial Museum of Natural History and Anthropology, 1964.

Fisher, Robin. *Contact and Conflict: Indian–European Relations in British Columbia, 1774–1890.* Vancouver: University of British Columbia Press, 1977.

Hawthorne, H. B., C. B. Belshaw, and S. M. Jamieson. *The Indians of British Columbia: A Study of Contemporary Social Adjustment.* Toronto: University of Toronto Press, 1958.

LaViolette, F. E. *The Struggle for Survival: Indian Cultures and the Protestant Ethic in British Columbia.* Toronto: University of Toronto Press, 1961.

Stanbury, W. T. *Success and Failure: Indians in Urban Society.* Vancouver: University of British Columbia Press, 1975.

The North

Berger, Thomas R. *Northern Frontier. Northern Homeland: The Report of the Mackenzie Valley Pipeline Inquiry.* Vol. 1. Ottawa: Supply and Services Canada, 1977.

Clark, A. M., ed. *Proceedings: Northern Athapaskan Conference, 1971.* 2 vols. Ottawa: National Museums of Canada, 1975.

Crowe, Keith J. *A History of the Original Peoples of Northern Canada.* Montreal: Arctic Institute of North America, 1974.

Fumoleau, René. *As Long As This Land Shall Last: A History of Treaty 8 and Treaty 11, 1870–1939.* Toronto: McClelland and Stewart, 1973.

McCullum, Hugh and Karmel, and John Olthuis. *Moratorium: Justice, Energy, the North, and the Native People.* Toronto: Anglican Book Centre, 1977.

Sissons, Jack. *Judge of the Far North: The Memoirs of Jack Sissons.* Toronto: McClelland and Stewart, 1968.

Vanstone, James W. *Athapaskan Adaptations. Hunters and Fishermen of the Subarctic Forests.* Chicago: Aldine, 1974.

Many articles on native subjects other than those listed can be found in back issues of:

Alberta History
BC Studies
Saskatchewan History
Transactions of the Historical and Scientific Society of Manitoba
Western Canadian Journal of Anthropology

Documentary Films:
A Selected List

For rental information write the respective distributors (listed below each entry). Documentaries produced by the National Film Board can be ordered from regional offices, or the head office in Ottawa.

Historical

"The Other Side of the Ledger: An Indian View of the Hudson's Bay Company"
42 minutes. Narrated by George Manuel, a former President of the National Indian Brotherhood.
NATIONAL FILM BOARD

"The Ballad of Crowfoot"
10 minutes. A short visual history of the opening of the Canadian West.
NATIONAL FILM BOARD

"Treaty with the Blackfoot"
28 minutes. An historical view of the background to, and the signing of, Treaty Seven.
GLENBOW–ALBERTA INSTITUTE
9th Avenue and 1st Street S.E.,
Calgary, Alberta T2G 0P3

"Tahtonka: Plains Indians' Buffalo Culture"
30 minutes. An historical review of the disappearance of the buffalo from Western North America.
MARLIN MOTION PICTURES
47 Lakeshore Road East,
Mississauga, Ontario

Plains Indians

"Circle of the Sun"
29 minutes. About the Blood Indians in the 1960's and their Sun Dance.
NATIONAL FILM BOARD.

"The Great Spirit"
28 minutes. A programme from C.B.C.'s "Man Alive" television series featuring Ernest Tootoosis, a descendant of Poundmaker, who explains the spiritual beliefs, rituals, stories, and songs of the Plains Cree.
NATIONAL FILM BOARD

"Kainai"
27 minutes. A documentary on the Blood Indians' pre-fabricated housing factory on their reserve near Cardston, Alberta.
NATIONAL FILM BOARD

"Starblanket"
27 minutes. A film about Noel Starblanket (currently—1978—the President of the National Indian Brotherhood), then chief of the Starblanket Reserve in Saskatchewan.
NATIONAL FILM BOARD

"Standing Buffalo"
23 minutes. An account of a Sioux (Dakota) rug-making co-operative on the Standing Buffalo Reserve in southern Saskatchewan.
NATIONAL FILM BOARD

"In the Spirit of Our Forefathers"
30 minutes. A film commemorating the signing of Treaty Six and the centennial ceremonies in 1976.
Audio Visual Department, SASKATCHEWAN INDIAN CULTURAL COLLEGE
P.O. Box 3085,
Saskatoon, Saskatchewan S4S 3S9

The Northern Indians

"The People at Dipper"
18 minutes. A documentary about the life of the Chipewyan Indians on a reserve in Northern Saskatchewan.
NATIONAL FILM BOARD

"I was Born Here"
24 minutes. A film produced by Father René Fumoleau, author of *As Long as This Land Shall Last*, about the Déné people of the Mackenzie River Valley.
MARLIN MOTION PICTURES
47 Lakeshore Road East,
Mississauga, Ontario

"Fort Good Hope"
47 minutes. Filmed during the Berger Inquiry. It presents the standpoint of the native peoples on the issue of land claims in the Mackenzie Valley.
NATIONAL FILM BOARD

The Indians of British Columbia

"In the Land of the War Canoes"
44 minutes. Photography pioneer Edward Curtis' classic film on the Kwakiutl Indians, recently re-edited in a sound version with the modern Kwakiutl speaking the lines of their ancestors and chanting their spells.
VIKING FILMS LTD.
525 Dennison Street,
Markham, Ontario L3R 1B8
or
UNIVERSITY OF WASHINGTON PRESS
Dept. of Audio-Visual,
110 Lewis Hall,
Seattle, Washington

"Potlatch. A Strict Law Bids Us Dance"
53 minutes. A study of the potlatch today, and the efforts of the federal government to suppress it in the early twentieth century.
PACIFIC CINEMATHEQUE
1616 West 3rd Avenue,
Vancouver, B.C. V6J 1K2

"Salmon People"
24 minutes. Compares an Indian legend about the salmon and the modern reality of Indian-owned fishing boats and canneries.
NATIONAL FILM BOARD

"This Land"
57 minutes. Reports on the efforts of the Nishga Indians in northern British Columbia to reclaim their land from the provincial government.
NATIONAL FILM BOARD

"The Shadowcatcher"
90 minutes. Shows the photographic work of Edward Curtis on the North American Indian. Integrated in the documentary is the film made in 1920 by Curtis among the tribes of the Northwest coast.
INTERNATIONAL TELE-FILM ENTERPRISES
47 Dersley Avenue,
Toronto, Ontario M6M 2P5

Contemporary

"People of the Sacred Circle"
27 minutes. A report on the Indian Ecumenical Conference held every year at the Stoney Reserve at Morley, Alberta.
NATIONAL FILM BOARD

"Cold Journey"
55 minutes. A film shot in Northern Manitoba and Saskatchewan about a young Indian's attempts to find himself. Relates his experiences in the "white man's" school.
NATIONAL FILM BOARD

"PowWow at Duck Lake"
14 minutes. A discussion at Duck Lake, Saskatchewan, of Indian–métis problems, particularly the educational programme offered native students.
NATIONAL FILM BOARD

"Mother of Many Children"
57 minutes. The story of a woman more than one hundred years old who lives on the Cree reserve at Hobbema, Alberta.
NATIONAL FILM BOARD

Native Art

"Colours of Pride"
30 minutes. Shows the work of four Indian artists—Norval Morrisseau, Allen Sapp, Daphne Odjig, Alex Janvier.
NATIONAL FILM BOARD

"By Instinct a Painter"
23 minutes. A film about the life and work of Allen Sapp, a Cree Indian from the Red Pheasant Reserve near North Battleford, Saskatchewan.
NATIONAL FILM BOARD

"Behind the Masks"
36 minutes. A look at the meaning behind the masks of British Columbia's coastal tribes by Claude Lévi-Strauss, the world-renowned anthropologist.
NATIONAL FILM BOARD

Notes on Contributors

HAROLD CARDINAL is a member of the Sucker Creek Indian band (Cree) in northern Alberta. After finishing high school in Edmonton, he studied sociology at Carleton University in Ottawa. Mr. Cardinal was elected president of the Indian Association of Alberta in 1968 and served nine consecutive terms in that position. He is the author of *The Unjust Society* (1969) and *The Rebirth of Canada's Indians* (1977).

JOSEPH E. COUTURE, of Cree background himself, taught high school in several native communities in Alberta before returning to university for further study. In 1972 he obtained his Ph.D. in educational psychology from the University of Alberta in Edmonton. A former director of research for the Indian Association of Alberta, he was one of the founders of the Alberta Indian Education Center. Since 1975 Professor Couture has been the chairman of the department of native studies at Trent University.

STAN CUTHAND, a member of the Little Pine Reserve (Plains Cree) in northern Saskatchewan, received his education on the reserve, went to high school in Prince Albert, and graduated in theology from Emmanuel College in Saskatoon in 1944. After his ordination in the Anglican Church, he served in parishes in both Saskatchewan and Alberta. Since 1975 Professor Cuthand has taught in the department of native studies at the University of Manitoba.

HUGH A. DEMPSEY was born in Edgerton, Alberta, and received his education in Edmonton. From 1956 to 1967 he served as archivist of the Glenbow Foundation and is presently the director of history of the Glenbow–Alberta Institute in Calgary. Mr. Dempsey is the author of *Crowfoot, Chief of the Blackfeet* and of numerous articles on Western Canada. In 1967 he was made an honourary chief of the Blood Indian band and currently serves as the secretary-treasurer of the Kainai Chieftainship, a select group of forty such honourary chiefs.

SELWYN DEWDNEY is a Canadian author and artist. He is the co-author of *Indian Rock Paintings of the Great Lakes* (1967) and the author of *They Shared to Survive. The Native Peoples of Canada* (1975) and *The Sacred Scrolls of the Southern Ojibway* (1975). He is now a full-time researcher into aboriginal pictographic media in Canada and a research associate in pictography at the Royal Ontario Museum.

ROGER GIBBINS has been teaching in the department of political science at the University of Calgary since 1973. He obtained his Ph.D. at Stanford University in 1974. Professor Gibbins has presented a number of papers on the recent nation-wide public opinion survey he conducted with Richard Ponting.

MARIE SMALLFACE MARULE, a member of the Blood tribe, received her education on reserve schools and at the University of Alberta in Edmonton where she studied sociology and anthropology. From 1966 to 1970 she taught as a CUSO volunteer in Zambia. Upon her return to Canada she worked with the National Indian Brotherhood in Ottawa, serving from 1973 to 1975 as the executive assistant to the president. She now teaches in the native American studies department at the University of Lethbridge.

E. PALMER PATTERSON II, presently an associate professor of history at the University of Waterloo, completed his Ph.D. thesis on "Andrew Paull and Canadian Indian Resurgence" at the University of Washington in 1962. Professor Patterson is the author of *The Canadian Indian: A History Since 1500* (1972).

J. RICK PONTING joined the department of sociology at the University of Calgary in 1973. He received his Ph.D. in that same year from Ohio State University. Recently he and Roger Gibbins completed a nation-wide study of public opinion toward Canadian Indians and contemporary Indian issues, and they have presented a number of joint papers on the survey.

ARTHUR J. RAY obtained his Ph.D. at the University of Wisconsin in Madison. Since 1971 he has taught geography at York University in Toronto. Professor Ray has published a number of articles on aspects of the early fur trade in Canada and is the author of *Indians in the Fur Trade* (1974).

JOHN SNOW, born and raised at Morley, Alberta, is chief of the Wesley Band of the Stoney Indians. He is also an ordained minister of the United Church of Canada. His history of the Stoneys, *These Mountains are Our Sacred Places*, appeared in 1977.

GEORGE F. G. STANLEY is one of Canada's most eminent historians. His first major publication, *The Birth of Western Canada: A History of the Riel Rebellions*, still in print today, was first published in 1936. A winner of the Royal Society's Tyrrell Medal, his numerous publications include *New France. The Last Phase, 1744–1760* (1968) and *Louis Riel* (1963).